WELCOME

When the iconic Hawker Siddeley Harrier entered service with Britain's Royal Air Force in 1969 it started a revolution in aerial combat. For the first time, a fighter jet could take off and land vertically, without the need for a runway. Almost immediately the Harrier was nicknamed the 'jump jet' and the name stuck. Once in the air, a Harrier had the performance of a fast jet and, as it demonstrated in the 1982 Falklands conflict, could hold its own against top-of-the-line enemy fighters. A legend was born.

Military pundits described the Harrier as a vertical take-off and landing (VTOL) or vertical and/or short take-off and landing (V/STOL) aircraft. Back in 1969, it was exclusively in service with the RAF. Soon after, other air arms spotted the potential of VTOL aircraft and either bought Harriers or developed their own jump jets. By the 1980s, India, Italy, Spain, the Soviet Union, and the United States Marine Corps were all operating jump jets.

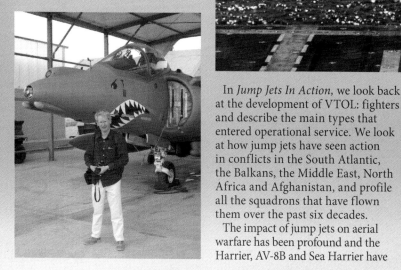

LEFT: The Harrier transformed how airpower operated from aircraft carriers. US DoD/Combat Camera

In *Jump Jets In Action*, we look back at the development of VTOL: fighters and describe the main types that entered operational service. We look at how jump jets have seen action in conflicts in the South Atlantic, the Balkans, the Middle East, North Africa and Afghanistan, and profile all the squadrons that have flown them over the past six decades.

The impact of jump jets on aerial warfare has been profound and the Harrier, AV-8B and Sea Harrier have all left their mark. A new-generation jump jet – the Lockheed Martin F-35B Lightning II – is now entering service in large numbers and looks set to create its own impact over decades to come.

We hope you find *Jump Jets In Action* an interesting read and lasting tribute to these great aircraft and the pilots that flew them.

Tim Ripley
Editor
March 2025

LEFT: Tim Ripley on tour with IV (AC) Squadron in Kuwait in April 2003 at the height of the invasion of Iraq. Tim Ripley

BELOW: US and British Harriers dominated the skies over Afghanistan. US DoD/Combat Camera

CONTENTS

ABOVE: The Harrier legend lives on through the heroic squadrons who pioneered VTOL operations in peace and war. US Navy

ABOVE: The F-35B Lightning II has picked up the baton from the Harrier as the jump jet for the 21st Century. US DoD/Combat Camera

The Harrier's distinctive shape is instantly recognisable. US DoD/Combat Camera

ABOVE: Spain is set to be the last-ever operator of the Harrier. Tim Felce

ABOVE: Since 1969 Harrier jump jets have delighted crowds at airshows with their aerial ballet displays. Tim Felce

ABOVE: Royal Navy Sea Harriers won the battle for air supremacy against Argentina during the 1982 Falklands conflict. MoD/Crown Copyright

ISBN: 978 1 83632 081 4
Editor: Tim Ripley
Data and photo research: Joseph Ripley
Senior editor, specials: Roger Mortimer
Email: roger.mortimer@keypublishing.com
Cover Design: Steve Donovan
Design: SJmagic DESIGN SERVICES, India
Advertising Sales Manager: Sam Clark
Email: sam.clark@keypublishing.com
Tel: 01780 755131
Advertising Production: Becky Antoniades
Email: Rebecca.antoniades@keypublishing.com

SUBSCRIPTION/MAIL ORDER
Key Publishing Ltd, PO Box 300, Stamford, Lincs, PE9 1NA
Tel: 01780 480404
Subscriptions email: subs@keypublishing.com

Mail Order email: orders@keypublishing.com
Website: www.keypublishing.com/shop

PUBLISHING
Group CEO and Publisher: Adrian Cox

Published by
Key Publishing Ltd, PO Box 100, Stamford, Lincs, PE9 1XQ
Tel: 01780 755131 **Website:** www.keypublishing.com

PRINTING
Precision Colour Printing Ltd, Haldane, Halesfield 1, Telford, Shropshire. TF7 4QQ

DISTRIBUTION
Seymour Distribution Ltd, 2 Poultry Avenue, London, EC1A 9PU
Enquiries Line: 02074 294000.

HOW JUMP JETS WORK

The revolutionary technology of VTOL combat aircraft

During the late 1940s and 1950s, many nations experimented with developing vertical take-off and landing (VTOL) jet combat aircraft in a bid to escape from dependence on runways. In the era of nuclear weapons, airfields were just too vulnerable when a single bomb could wipe out a fully equipped airbase in a matter of seconds. A VTOL jet could operate from remote sites, hidden from aerial surveillance in forests or factories. Navies also liked the idea of putting fast jets to sea without having to build large and expensive aircraft carriers.

Helicopters were starting to enter service in large numbers during the 1950s and they were showing considerable potential in conflicts in Korea, Indochina, Algeria and during the 1956 Suez crisis. This was a time of great strides in aviation technology and designers around the world were scrambling to produce workable solutions to create VTOL jets.

Some of the ideas put forward were the jet-powered Rolls-Royce 'Flying Bedstead', the Convair XFY Pogo – which combined jets with propellers – and the Dornier Do 31 jet cargo aircraft. Several of these designs showed potential, being able to rise vertically off the ground and

LEFT: The British-designed Harrier was the original jump jet and led to the development of a whole family of VTOL aircraft. MoD/Crown Copyright

LEFT: The Hawker P.1127 prototype proved that the unique nozzle system worked, allowing the rapid development of the Harrier from 1965. John Chapman

BELOW: The Royal Navy showed interest in the P.1127, but it was the RAF that moved it into service. Mike Freer

hover but transitioning to level flight proved a major hurdle that few of these concepts could overcome.

The key breakthrough was made in the late 1950s by French aircraft designer, Michel Wilbault, who proposed using four separate compressors or nozzles powered by an Orion powerplant made by the Bristol Engine Company. He produced the idea of using four rotating exhaust nozzles that could be turned using shafting and gearboxes to create the lift needed to get the aircraft off the ground. The pilot then used a control in the cockpit to swivel the nozzles into horizontal position to propel the aircraft forward. It was a simple and effective design that was subsequently incorporated into the Harrier by Hawker Aviation. It was the first truly effective VTOL technology, which allowed the Harrier to be stable in vertical fight and then smoothly transition to level fight. The Harrier would delight airshow audiences by bowing its nose to crowds while hovering and flying backwards.

The Bristol Engine Company eventually became part of Rolls-Royce, and its VTOL engine was dubbed the Pegasus. Hawker Aviation had been merged into Hawker Siddeley by the time Harrier entered serial production in the late 1960s. Custodianship of the Harrier subsequently passed to the nationalised British Aircraft Corporation (BAC) in the 1970s and then British Aerospace (BAe) after it returned to private ownership a decade later. After 1999, the final versions of the Harrier were the responsibility of BAE Systems.

The essential elements of the Harrier design were proved on the P.1127 prototype which first lifted off the ground in November 1960 at the company's site in Dunsfold, Surrey, which later became the centre of Harrier production. The first

conventional take-off took place the following year and more complicated evolutions of the VTOL fight envelope were tested.

Britain, West Germany, and the United States joined forces in 1961 to order nine prototypes, known as the Kestrel, and these began flight testing from March 1964 under a multi-national project office. Test flights discovered that the endurance and weapon-carrying capacity of the aircraft could be dramatically improved if a short rolling take-off was used to gain forward momentum before the pilot started to move the nozzles into the vertical take-off position. This technique became known as vertical and/or short take-off and landing (V/STOL) and it allowed jump jets to operate from very short runways, dirt air strips, roads, or small aircraft carriers.

At that stage, the Americans and Germans did not decide to buy jump jets, but the RAF was keen to acquire them as a replacement for its main ground attack jet, the Hawker Hunter. It proposed a supersonic jump jet that was named the Hawker P.1154 Harrier, but this was cancelled in 1965 on cost grounds. The go-ahead was given to build a subsonic jump jet, which retained the name Harrier. Externally, it looked very similar »

LEFT: The P.1127 and then the Harrier had four rotating exhaust nozzles that allowed the pilot to direct thrust downwards to allow the aircraft to lift off vertically.
Alan Wilson

LEFT: A multinational effort built the Kestrel testbed aircraft, but only Britain decided to move the aircraft into production as the Harrier.
Clemens Vasters

BELOW: The Harrier's Pegasus engine was an integral element of the aircraft and could only be removed by lifting off the one-piece wing section.
MoD/Crown Copyright

to the P.1127 and the Kestrel, but its internal mechanical and electronic systems were far more mature and were considered combat-ready.

At the same time as the British were perfecting the Harrier, the Soviet Navy was in the market for a jump jet to operate from its first generation of aircraft carriers. Lacking the size to incorporate the catapults and arresting hooks needed to operate fast jets in the US and British style, the Soviet Kiev-class carriers required a VTOL fighter. The Yakovlev Design Bureau came up with a very different way of generating vertical lift. They combined a Tumansky R-28 V-300 jet engine that provided the forward power with two Rybinsk (RKBM) RD-38s fixed just behind the cockpit to provide the vertical lift. Additional stability was provided by a rotating exhaust nozzle for the Tumansky engine and ducting out to the wingtips and tail. The jet had five sources of upward lift, which ensured it remained stable during VTOL manoeuvres.

The Yakovlev Yak-38 (NATO: Forger) proved very challenging to fly, as the pilot had to manually juggle all the different forms of vertical lift during take-offs and landings. It had an automatic ejection seat, so that if one of the take-off engines failed or the aircraft rolled past 60°, the pilot was automatically ejected from the aircraft.

The Yak-38 saw service from the mid-1970s to end of the Soviet Union in 1991, but no other nation copied the idea or bought the aircraft. A supersonic evolution, the Yak-141, was under development in the late 1980s and four prototypes were built, but the project was scrapped when the Berlin Wall fell, bringing jump jet development in Russia to an end.

In the 1990s, Britain and America were both keen to develop a successor to their Harriers, joining forces to work on a V/STOL variant that was initially called the Joint Strike Fighter (JSF). This was meant to replace the Lockheed F-16 Fighting Falcon and Fairchild A-10 Warthog attack jets of the USAF, the US Navy's, and US

Marine Corps McDonnell Douglas F/A-18 Hornets, as well the AV-8Bs, Harriers and Sea Harriers of the US Marine Corps, RAF, and Royal Navy. Land, carrier and V/STOL F-35 variants were developed to meet all these requirements.

US aerospace giants McDonnell Douglas, Northrop, Lockheed, and Boeing all threw their hats in the ring and offered different solutions for the jump jet variant of the JSF. McDonnell Douglas proposed an aircraft powered by a reheated turbofan, with a remote gas-driven fan to augment lift in

the V/STOL mode, a configuration called Gas-Driven Lift Fan (GDLF). The Northrop aircraft featured an auxiliary lift engine augmenting the dry thrust from a reheated turbofan fitted with a pair of thrust-vectoring nozzles, referred to as Lift-Plus-Lift/ Cruise (LPLC). The Lockheed concept used a reheated turbofan with thrust augmentation from a remote shaft-driven lift fan known as the Shaft-Driven Lift Fan (SDLF), eventually leading to the Pratt & Whitney YF119-PW-611, which powered what became the X-35B JSF demonstrator. Boeing decided against thrust augmentation and proposed an aircraft powered by a reheated turbofan that could be reconfigured into a direct lift engine with a pair of thrust-vectoring nozzles positioned in the centre of aircraft.

Boeing's X-32 and Lockheed Martin's X-35 made the cut to the final stage of the JSF competition. Britain's BAE was allowed to join both teams, but the Boeing solution was considered the direct technological descendent of the Harrier and its rotating lift nozzles.

In the end, the Pentagon thought the Lockheed F-35 and its lift fan solution

ABOVE: McDonnell Douglas advanced the Harrier design by developing a new wing made of advanced composite material, which reduced weight and improved lift. Michael Pereckas

LEFT: The Rolls-Royce Pegasus engines was progressively enhanced to improve its performance and reduce manufacturing costs. Jay Pee

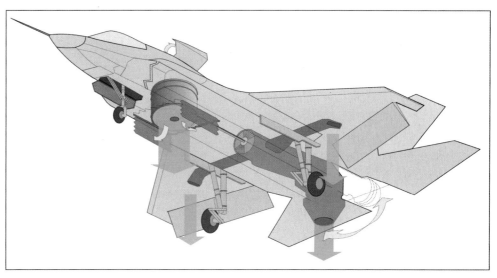

was the most effective way to take V/STOL flight into the 21st Century, saying the higher performance of the Lockheed Martin lift fan system was worth the extra risk. When near to the ground, the Boeing X-32 suffered from the problem of hot air from the exhaust circulating back to the main engine, which caused the thrust to weaken and the engine to overheat.

The selection of the Lockheed Martin F-35 Lightning II for the JSF project ended more than 40 years of British leadership in VTOL aircraft design. BAE System, Rolls-Royce and other British companies gained nearly 20% workshare on the F-35, but the project is led by the United States and American aerospace companies control the design. Rolls-Royce engineers in Bristol were involved in designing the lift-fan for Pratt & Whitney, but once the engine entered production, the Rolls-Royce site in

Indianapolis won the work to build the gearbox, clutch, driveshaft, and nozzle and conducted the build and verification testing of the F-35 lift-fan.

The F-35B variant is now the sole V/STOL combat aircraft in production and in operational use around the world. It is set to remain on the frontline well into the 2050s, when the world might very well be looking for a new generation of jump jets.

TOP: The Rolls-Royce lift fan powers the F-35B into vertical flight. Tosaka

ABOVE: A rotating rear exhaust is part of the F-35's vertical lift fan design. US DoD

LEFT: The Pratt & Whitney F119-PW-611 engine powers the F-35B in forward flight. Steve Jurvetson

HARRIER GR1/3

The original jump jet

Once the British government confirmed its order for the Harrier in 1965, the Hawker team under chief designer John Fozzard began work to refine the concept for production.

The first prototype Hawker Siddeley Harrier GR1 took to the skies over Dunsfold airfield in August 1966 and the first production order was placed with Hawker Siddeley in December 1967. Ultimately, the RAF ordered 118 Harriers, with deliveries from Dunsfold continuing into the early 1980s.

The Harrier GR1 incorporated many refinements from the P.1127 and Kestrel

prototypes, including significant enhancements to the Pegasus engine and the nozzle system to control the aircraft during vertical take-off and landing (VTOL). A modified wing design was incorporated, with a slightly smaller wing area but an increased span. Each wing had two hard points for stores, two of which were plumbed to allow drop tanks of additional fuel to be carried. Under the fuselage were two attaching points for strakes or 30mm Aden cannon pods, as well as a centre line pylon.

The fuselage was made of a mixture of aluminium and titanium, with the latter material being used in sections that would be in contact with hot jet blasts or engine components. The Pegasus 6 engine was a revolutionary design incorporating an all-titanium fan and other components made of

lightweight heat resistant materials. The four VTOL nozzles were controlled by dual motors aligned by a mechanism to ensure they all moved simultaneously. Each of the nozzles were fitted with moveable shutters that allowed the pilot to fine-tune his hover manoeuvres. To ease the pilot's workload during VTOL flight, the Harrier incorporated an auto-stabilisation system to help control the nozzles and their shutters.

The RAF envisaged using the Harrier GR1 as a ground attack aircraft, so it was not built with an air-to-air radar. It was optimised for close air support operations, so was given a Ferranti FE541 internal navigation system linked to a moving map display in the aircraft's cockpit. This revolutionary device allowed the pilot to pinpoint his position without having to consult

a paper map, which was a major help for pilots trying to find small targets while flying at low level. It was also fitted with a head-up display (HUD), which projected key flight information and weapon aiming information onto a glass plate just inside the front window of the cockpit. As a result, a Harrier pilot could fly the aircraft without having to look down into his cockpit. Although HUDs are now a standard feature of modern combat aircraft, in the 1960s they were only starting to be introduced, so the Harrier was a trail blazer.

Training pilots to fly the Harrier was a major challenge as its unique VTOL technology was not at all like flying a helicopter, so required a dedicated training variant. The RAF ordered 25 two-seaters, designated T2s and T4s. »

ABOVE: Harrier GR3 variants featured a nose-mounted laser ranger and marked target seeker to allow forward air controllers to rapidly pinpoint ground targets.
Tony Higsett

BELOW: The Harrier GR1 was recognisable from its 'pointed' nose configuration.
Mike Freer

ABOVE: 1 (F) Fighter Squadron had a global role, including operating in the Arctic north of Norway, requiring improvised snow camouflage scheme to be applied.
Wilsthirespotter

LEFT: Two squadrons of the RAF Harrier Force were based on Germany for nearly 30 years as part of NATO frontline defences.
Wilsthirespotter

The Harrier was an immediate success, and the RAF was keen to improve its performance and capabilities. To allow forward air controllers on the ground to pinpoint targets with a laser designator, Harrier GR3s were fitted with a Ferranti Type 106 laser ranger and marked target seeker (LRMTS). This projected an icon on the aircraft's HUD, allowing the pilot to rapidly bring his weapon to bear on a ground target. The LRMTS sensor was installed in a housing fitted to the nose of the GR3 to replace the pitot probe, which makes it easy to distinguish between the GR1 and GR3 variants.

LEFT: The Rock of Gibraltar provided a backdrop for a training deployment of a Harrier GR3 of 233 Operational Conversion Unit.
Pete Butt

HAWKER SIDDELEY HARRIER GR3	
Length	14.27m (46ft 10in)
Wingspan	7.7m (25ft 3in)
Max take-off weight	11,430kg (25,200lb)
Max speed	1,175 kph (730 mph)
Range/combat radius	670km (415miles)
Armament	Two 30mm Aden cannon, four Sidewinder air-to-air missiles, 72 SNEB rockets in four pods, various combinations of munitions including Paveway laser-guided bombs and BL755 cluster bombs and reconnaissance pod.

The GR3 also featured a Pegasus 11/Mk103 engine, which generated more thrust and enabled the aircraft to carry more weapons, as well as extending the time between overhauls. A radar warming receiver (RWRs) to alert pilots to enemy radar threats was fitted as standard.

From the start, the RAF wanted its Harriers to focus on close air support operations in Germany for the British Army of the Rhine (BOAR). It developed a concept of field deployment to exploit the aircraft's unique VTOL capabilities, with Harriers operating from camouflaged hides or factory buildings to confuse enemy aerial reconnaissance. A joint RAF/Royal Engineers support organisation was set up to disperse fuel supplies, repairs, ammunition, and photographic interpretation to field locations.

The British government was keen to recoup its investment in building the Harrier by winning export orders. A number of promotional activities were staged to show of the aircraft's unique capabilities. A Harrier pilot was entered in the *Daily Mail*'s transatlantic race in May 1969, to commemorate the 50th anniversary of the first Atlantic crossing by aviation pioneers John Alcock and Arthur Brown. The aim was to see who could get from the top of the Post Office Tower in London to the viewing platform of the Empire State Building in New York in as short a time as possible. The shortest overall time from London to New York was by Squadron Leader Tom Lecky-Thompson in an RAF Harrier, clocking in at six hours and 11 minutes. He took off from a coal yard next to St Pancras station in London and landed at Bristol Basin on the East River in New York, using air-to-air refuelling on a number of occasions over the North Atlantic.

Over the next 40 years, British Harrier pilots would write more new chapters in aviation history.

AV-8A

America's jump jet

The Harrier's first export success was in America after the US Congress approved the purchase of the aircraft for the US Marine Corps (USMC) in September 1969.

With America embroiled in the Vietnam conflict, the USMC was keen to exploit the Harrier's unique VTOL capabilities during amphibious landings, alongside its expanding fleet of helicopters. It was starting to bring a fleet of dedicated helicopter carriers, known as amphibious assault ships, into service as power projection platforms and saw the Harrier as a way to put fixed wing airpower ashore on beachheads without requiring airfields to be captured or runways to be built, as was needed for its existing Douglas A-4 Skyhawk light attack jets.

It was only due to the enthusiastic and determined lobbying by the USMC leadership that political reluctance to buying a foreign aircraft could be overcome. However, the initial order was not big enough for a dedicated assembly line to be set up in the United States for the McDonnell Douglas AV-8A, as the Harrier was designated in USMC service. As a result, the aircraft were built at Dunsfold and airfreighted to America, where McDonnell Douglas fitted the wings before flight testing. Ultimately, the USMC bought 110 AV-8Bs, including eight TAV-8As, with deliveries taking place between 1971 and 1976.

The USMC aircraft were essentially the same as RAF GR1s, but fitted with US-sourced radios, identification-friend-or-foe (IFF) systems and a navigation/attack system. The Pegasus 11 engine was

designated the F402-RR-402 by the USMC, and the weapon suite included a range of US ordnance, including Rockeye II cluster bombs and 500lb Mk 81/82 and 1,000lb Mk 83 free fall bombs.

Eventually three Marine Attack Squadrons (VMAs) and an operational conversion unit were equipped with the AV-8A. The USMC used its jump jets in many tactical

experiments during training exercises in the 1970s and 1980s, including flying them off merchant ships, but they never saw combat. Between 1979 and 1984, the USMC upgraded 47 aircraft to the AV-8C configuration, with enhanced avionics and structural improvements.

The American purchase proved instrumental in the sale of the Harrier to the Spanish Navy.

ABOVE: VMA-513 was the first operational USMC squadron, receiving its initial jets in 1971. USMC

BELOW: The USMC regularly deployed its Harriers to Norway to support NATO defences in the Arctic. USMC

USMC AV-8As routinely embarked on US Navy amphibious assault ships as part of marine expeditionary units. USMC

Technically, Britain had banned arms sales to Franco's fascist regime, so could not sell the aircraft direct to Madrid. Nevertheless, a Harrier was successfully demonstrated to the Spanish in 1972 and, the following year, an order was placed for jets to be used on the aircraft carrier, SPS *Dadelo*. To get around the export ban, the aircraft were built at Dunsfold and flown to the US for final assembly, where the Spanish crews were being trained by the USMC. The 11 single-seat aircraft were dubbed AV-8S Matadors and a pair of two-seater TAV-8As were also ordered. All the aircraft were built to a similar configuration as USMC jets. A first batch was delivered in 1976, with a second order fulfilled in 1980.

Although the AV-8As never saw action, the USMC studied the aircraft and incorporated many lessons learned in an enhanced jump jet that would be designed and built by McDonnell Douglas in St Louis.

McDONNELL DOUGLAS AV-8A HARRIER	
Length	14.27m (46ft 10in)
Wingspan	7.7m (25ft 3in)
Max take-off weight	11,430kg (25,200lb)
Max speed	1,175kph (730mph)
Range/combat radius	670km (415miles)
Armament	Two 30mm Aden cannon, two AIM-9G Sidewinder air-to-air missiles, Rockeye II or Snakeye cluster bombs, 500lb Mk 81/82 and 1,000lb Mk 83 free fall bombs, four Zuni rocket pods, Mk 77 napalm bombs.

ABOVE: Once the USMC received its first two-seat TAV-8A trainers, the number of fatal accidents during conversion training reduced dramatically. USMC

LEFT: Air-to-air refuelling from KC-130s tanker/transports allowed the USMC to deploy its AV-8A rapidly around the world. USMC

SEA HARRIER FRS1/FA2

The jump jet in Royal Navy service

RIGHT: The FA2 was the definitive variant of the Sea Harrier, which entered service from 1994.
MoD/Crown Copyright

BELOW: The Sea Harrier was developed in the 1970s to operate from the new Invincible-class 'through deck cruisers'.
MoD/Crown Copyright

Royal Navy interest in the Harrier jump jet was late in developing due to the Admiralty's attempts to try to keep its catapult and arrestor wire-equipped aircraft carriers in service. It was only once plans to build a successor to its 'cats and traps' carriers were firmly quashed by the Labour government in 1966 that the Fleet Air Arm started to take the Harrier seriously.

In 1973, the Royal Navy ordered the first of three Invincible-class aircraft carriers. The last of the 'cats and traps' carriers, HMS *Ark Royal,* was to be retired in 1978, so the Fleet Air Arm was now accelerating efforts to find a suitable jet fighter for its new class of carriers. They were initially dubbed 'through deck cruisers' to overcome political objections to big carriers.

Hawker Siddeley received a study contract to develop a 'navalised' version of the Harrier GR1/3. As the Royal Navy wanted its new fighter to be a fleet air defence aircraft, a key requirement was for it to have a radar that could detect both aircraft and ships. Ferranti developed the Blue Fox pulse-modulated I-band radar for the Sea Harrier from the Sea Spray radar used on the Lynx maritime helicopter.

For the naval variant of the Harrier the cockpit was raised by 10cm to improve pilot visibility. Another important change was to replace all magnesium components in the Pegasus Mk104 engine to prevent salt-water corrosion. The aircraft had to be a multi-role, fighter, reconnaissance, and strike jet, so it was designated the FRS1. To carry out the reconnaissance mission »

a single F95 oblique camera was mounted in the nose.

The Sea Harrier's main air-to-air armament was the US-made AIM-9 Sidewinder heat-seeking missile. Two could be carried on the outer pylons. Air-to-grounds weapons included 1,000lb or 2,000lb iron or 'dumb' bombs and the Sea Eagle

anti-ship guided missile could also be deployed.

During the development of the Sea Harrier and the building of the Invincible-class carriers, it was discovered that rolling take-offs were far more fuel efficient than direct vertical ascents. This was helped even further by a new British invention

dubbed the 'ski jump': a 12° ramp at the end of the carrier's flight jet, which meant the Sea Harrier could take off with a significantly enhanced payload, allowing it to stay on station for longer. The three Invincible-class carriers and HMS *Hermes* were fitted with ski jumps to accommodate Sea Harrier operations.

An initial order for 24 Sea Harrier FRS1s was placed in May 1975. Eventually 57 Sea Harriers were built, along with three navalised two-seat T4N trainers, which did not have the Blue Fox radar.

The Sea Harrier was an instant success. It proved to be rugged, reliable and was credited with playing a major part in winning the 1982 Falklands conflict, where the jets flew air defence, ground attack and reconnaissance missions. Twenty-eight Sea Harriers went to the South Atlantic with the British task force and six were lost, two to Argentinian ground fire and four in accidents.

During the 1980s, the Soviet naval threat in the North Atlantic escalated, with the deployment of supersonic Tupolev Tu-22M3 *Backfire* bombers armed with long-range anti-ship missiles and the appearance of Yakovlev Yak-38 *Forger* carrier-borne jump jets. To counter these new threats, the Royal Navy pushed for an upgrade to the Sea Harrier to allow it to fire beyond-visual-range air-to-air missiles.

The contract for development of the Sea Harrier FA2 for fighter attack was placed with BAE in 1985 and the first prototype flew in 1988. The FA2 featured a new radar, the Ferranti

Blue Vixen pulse-doppler, mounted in a new nosecone. This made the FA2 the first European aircraft to be equipped to carry the new US AIM-120 advanced medium air-to-air missile (AMRAAM), which allowed tit to engage targets at a range of up to 100 kilometres.

A production contract for the conversion of 31 FRS1s into FA2s was confirmed in December 1988 and a further 10 new-build aircraft were ordered in 1990. The conversions were scheduled to take place between 1991 and 1994, with the new aircraft scheduled for delivery in 1994. However, the project »

BELOW: All of the three Invincible-class carriers and HMS *Hermes* were fitted with ski jumps.
MoD/Crown Copyright

was hit by technical problems in integrating the radar and deliveries of the AIM-120s from America were also delayed. As a result, the first converted aircraft was not delivered until June 1993, while the first new-build FA2 was handed over in October 1995. Production did not end until December 1998.

The FA2 remained in service until another round of defence cuts in 2004 called time on the last of the Sea Harriers. All the jets were retired by 2006 and the Fleet Air Arm fast jet squadrons switched to flying the Harrier GR7/9 used by the RAF. This forced the Fleet Air Arm to focus on ground attack and give up the air superiority/fleet defence role. The Sea Harrier would be the Royal Navy's last true fighter jet.

Hawker Siddeley and the British government were keen to win export orders for their maritime jump jet and dispatched a two-seat Harrier demonstrator around the world. In 1972, the Harrier landed on the Indian carrier INS *Vikrant*. Seven years later, the Indian Navy placed an order for its first six Sea Harriers, which were dubbed FRS51s, along with two T4N two-seat trainers. They were essentially the same as the Royal Navy's jets,

except for different radios and identification-friend-or-foe (IFF) systems. The Indians were not able to buy AIM-9 Sidewinders from the US, so their jets were fitted with French-made Matra R.550 Magic heat-seeking missiles. Subsequently, Israeli missiles were acquired for the Indian Navy jets. A ski jump was eventually fitted to INS *Vikrant* to improve the performance of her Sea Harriers. In total, India bought 23 FRS51s and four T4N trainers. The jets remained in service until 2016, when they were replaced by Russian-supplied Mikoyan MiG-29Ks.

Export campaigns in Italy, Australia and Spain failed to generate orders. The Australians

wanted the jets after the British government put HMS *Invincible* up for sale in 1981 as part of a round of defence cuts. This sale was cancelled after the Falklands conflict, so the Australians had little need for the Sea Harriers. Meanwhile, Italy and Spain opted for the radar-equipped McDonnell Douglas AV-8B Harrier II Plus.

The Sea Harrier was the last all-British fighter jet to enter service, and it proved to be a highly effective aircraft, winning its spurs in the Falklands. But by the 21st Century, it was showing its age and the Royal Navy decided to opt for the American Lockheed Martin F-35B Lightning II as its future carrier borne aircraft.

ABOVE: The Sea Harrier FA2 was designed to employ AIM-120 AMRAAMs so the jet could engage aerial targets beyond visual range.
MoD/Crown Copyright

SEA HARRIER FRS1	
Length	14.5m (47ft 7in)
Wingspan	7.69m (25ft 3in)
Max take-off weight	11,339kg (25,000lb)
Max speed	1,188kph (642kts)
Combat range	463km (250nm), fighter role 740km (400nm)
Armament	Two 30mm Aden cannon, four Sidewinder air-to-air missiles, various combinations of bombs or two Sea Eagle air-to-surface missiles

YAK-38

Carrier air power for the USSR

The Soviet Union responded to the development of jump jets in the early 1960s by looking into the aircraft that became known as the Yakovlev Yak-38. It was intended to operate from a new class of aircraft carriers that entered service in the mid-1970s. The prototype flew for the first time in 1970, and the initial production model was built a year later. The initial pre-production version had been designated the Yak-36M, but once the aircraft entered production it was renamed the Yak-38. The Yak-38 formally

YAKOVLEV YAK-38M	
Length	16.37m (53ft 8in)
Wingspan	7.32m (24ft)
Max take-off weight	11,300kg (24,912lb)
Max speed	1,050kph (650mph)
Range	1,300km (810miles)
Armament	One or two GSh-23L 23 mm gun pods, various types of rockets (up to 240 mm) Two anti-ship or air-to-surface Kh-23 (AS-7 Kerry) and R-60 or R-60M (AA-8 Aphid) air-to-air missiles. Two FAB-500 or four FAB-250 general-purpose bombs, two incendiary ZB-500s or two nuclear RN-28 bombs.

entered service in 1976 and 231 were built, including prototypes and two-seat trainers.

The Yak-38s vertical lift system was unique to the aircraft, incorporating vertically mounted jet engines, rotating exhaust nozzles and wing-mounted exhaust ducts. An upgraded version, the Yak-38M, featured more powerful engines. It first entered service in 1985 and was dubbed the *Forger-A* by NATO. Thirty-eight two-seat trainers, the Yak-38Us *Forger-B*, were built between 1978 and 1981.

After the collapse of the Soviet Union in 1991, the Yak-38s were withdrawn from service and scrapped. Although the type never saw combat, its appearance caused a stir with western naval powers because of its arsenal of heat-seeking air-to-air missiles and laser-guided air-to-surface missiles. It prompted the Royal Navy upgrade the Sea Harrier, which became the FA2 variant.

ABOVE: The Yak-38 was designed to be embarked on the Soviet Navy's three Kiev-class aircraft carriers. US Navy

LEFT: The Yak-38 employed two vertically mounted engines to provide lift. Vladimir Rodionov

BELOW: The Soviet Navy's Northern and Pacific fleets were each assigned a Yak-38 regiment to support their carrier operations. Rob Schleiffert

Once the US Marine Corps (USMC) got its hands on its first AV-8A in the early 1970s, it immediately realised the potential of the jump jet to transform the way it operated. It asked for a bigger and better version of the Harrier that had more range, greater payload, and better avionics.

In co-operation with the engineers at McDonnell Douglas in St Louis, USMC officers came up with proposals for an improved jump jet that looked a lot like the old AV-8A but was essentially a completely new aircraft. McDonnell Douglas teamed up with Hawker Siddeley to work on the AV-16A Advanced

Harrier, which was intended to have double the range and payload of the old AV-8A. The concept revolved around development of a more

powerful engine with an increased diameter fan, the Pegasus 15, and an advanced wing

The British pulled out of the project in 1975, when the estimated $250 million cost of developing the new engine proved unaffordable. This left the Americans to push ahead alone to build the aircraft that became known as the McDonnell Douglas AV-8B Harrier II.

Central to the AV-8B was the redesigned wing, made predominately out of composite materials. The aircraft's wings were built as a single component that had to be lifted off the fuselage to change the engine. At the time it was the largest airframe component ever manufactured in epoxy resin composite, which promised to be corrosion-proof, fatigue-resistant and 400% stronger than a comparative alloy wing. It required the creation of new manufacturing processes to laminate together sheets of material.

LEFT: The AV-8B sported a new wing to boost lift and an elevated cockpit to improve the pilot's view during close air support missions. US DoD/Combat Camera

BELOW: The Harrier II retained the four exhaust nozzle system found on earlier variants, but digital engine control systems reduced pilot workload. D Miller

AV-8B
A jump jet for the US Marines

The wing design had a slightly reduced sweepback but was thicker and had an increased span. Bigger fuel tanks could be fitted to it, giving the jet the equivalent of a further 30 minutes on station. There were metal wingtips, leading edges, and outrigger attachment points, while larger flaps were fitted to increase the lift. The outrider wheels were also moved closer to the fuselage.

To accommodate the larger Pegasus Mk105 engine, the fuselage had to be expanded, and the cockpit was raised to give the pilot a better view out of the side of the aircraft. This meant the rear fuselage had to be extended to maintain the aircraft's centre of gravity and composite materials were used to reduce weight. The new engine was fitted with a digital flight control system, which considerably eased pilot workload and improved fuel efficiency. To improve the vertical take-off performance, the exhaust nozzles were redesigned to help focus the downwash under the aircraft.

Considerable effort was put into enhancing the AV-8B's avionics and attack systems. The cockpit was fitted with multi-function displays to show flight and combat information, as well as hands-off throttle and stick (HOTAS) controls. A mission computer and attack system allowed the pilot to put bombs accurately on target in dive attacks. Radar warning receivers and chaff/flare dispensers were fitted as standard, as well as a provision for jamming pods. The AV-8B was fitted with GAU-12/A Equalizer Gatling gun pods, to replace the British-sourced 30mm Aden cannons used on the AV-8As. A two-seat version, the TAV-8B, was built to help train USMC pilots.

Work on prototypes gathered pace in 1979 until full scale development was authorised, with the first hover tests taking place in 1981. The following year, the first batch of 12 production aircraft were ordered, and the jet formally entered service with the USMC in December 1983, to allow the first unit, VMA-331, to be declared operational in January 1985. The AV-8B remained in production until 1995 for the USMC and the Italian and Spanish navies, with 323 being built, including 262 single-seaters and 22 two-seaters for training.

The USMC began to look to improve the AV-8B in 1989, incorporating ❯❯

ABOVE: Italy and Spain were export customers for the AV-8B Plus and both navies fitted ski jumps to their carriers. The US Navy did not fit ski jumps to their amphibious assault ships. Aldo Bidini

LEFT: The two-seat TAV-8B was developed to provide training for Harrier II pilots. US DoD/ Combat Camera

a forward looking infrared (FLIR) night-vision system in the nose. This new variant was known as the AV-8B (Night Attack), which also featured cockpit modifications to allow the pilot to use night-vision goggles (NVGs). It also featured the enhanced F402-RR-408 engine. These improvements were incorporated on the St Louis production line from the 88th aircraft.

The next major upgrade was the fitting of a Hughes AN/APG-65 pulse-doppler radar to give the jet an air-to-air capability, with the AIM-120 AMRAAM for beyond visual range engagements. This was in addition to the night-attack capabilities incorporated in the AV-8A (NA) variant. It also had the same wing used in RAF GR5/7 variants, which had four additional wing pylons.

These new aircraft were dubbed the AV-8B Harrier II Plus or AV-8B Plus. It was originally planned to build 55 of them and convert 192 existing aircraft to the new configuration, but the end of the Cold War led to budget cuts, and the programme was scaled back dramatically. Only 42 new-build aircraft were ordered and 74 old airframes converted. In the 21st century, enhancements to the aircraft included the addition of the Litening II targeting pods to allow the jets to carry laser-guided bombs.

Once the Harrier II had a meaningful air-to-air capability, the Spanish, and

LEFT: For more than 40 years, the AV-8B was the workhorse of USMC attack aviation squadrons. US DoD/ Combat Camera

BELOW LEFT: USMC Harriers perform rolling take-offs from amphibious assault ships to improve the jump jet's performance. US DoD/Combat Camera

McDONNELL DOUGLAS AV-8B HARRIER II PLUS	
Length	14.12m (46ft 4in)
Wingspan	9.25m (30ft 4in)
Max take-off weight	10,410kg (22,950lb)
Max speed	1,083kph (673mph)
Combat range	556km (350miles)
Armament	One General Dynamics GAU-12 Equalizer 25 mm (0.984 in) five-barrelled rotary cannon mounted under-fuselage in a pod. Four Zuni pods for 76 Hydra 70/APKWS 70 mm rockets Four AIM-9 Sidewinder or AIM-120 AMRAAMs, four AGM-65 E/F Maverick missiles. Assorted bombs, including CBU-100/Mk 20 Rockeye II cluster bombs, Mark 81, 82 or 83 unguided bombs, GBU-12 or GBU-16 laser-guided bombs, GBU-38, GBU-32 or GBU-54 joint direct attack munitions, Mk 77 napalm bombs.

Italians both decided to place orders for the AV-8B Plus variant instead of Sea Harrier FA2s. This allowed the Spanish to sell off their old AV-8S Matadors to Thailand. Meanwhile, the Italians ordered 16 AV-8B Plus aircraft, along with a pair of two-seat trainers in 1989. The Spanish had ordered 12 AV-8Bs in 1983 and added eight AV-8B Plus and a TAV-8B in 1990.

Unlike the AV-8A, which never saw combat, the AV-8B was destined to become the workhorse of USMC tactical aviation combat operations over 40 years, at its peak in 1990 equipping eight front-line marine attack squadrons. The AV-8B is in the process of being phased out in favour of the Lockheed Martin F-35B Lightning II, with only two squadrons currently flying the AV-8B.

LEFT: The AV-8B has proved to be a robust and easy to maintain aircraft on both ships and shore, requiring significantly fewer numbers of maintainers than other fixed wing combat aircraft.
US DoD/Combat Camera

BELOW: US AV-8Bs have taken part in every foreign war and intervention by America from 1991 to date, providing stalwart support to USMC ground units.
US DoD/Combat Camera

GR5 TO GR9

The RAF's next-generation jump jet

The GR9 was the final British variant of the jump jet, and its extensive weapons suite made it 'the ultimate Harrier' for RAF and Fleet Air Arm pilots.
MoD/Crown Copyright

When the British pulled out of the AV-16A project in 1975, the RAF and Ministry of Defence had to rethink how to replace the old Harrier GR3s. Hawker Siddeley was tasked to produce a cheaper way to produce a second-generation Harrier. The fatigue life of the RAF's Harriers was being used up at a very fast rate and it was estimated that the entire fleet would need to be taken out of service by the end of the 1980s.

The design team at Hawker Siddeley's Kingston site had the same idea as their counterparts at McDonnell Douglas and proposed fitting the GR3 with a bigger wing, but unlike the US project, it would be made from metal rather than composites and was dubbed the 'tin wing'. Many features, including the raised cockpit used on the Sea Harriers, were proposed for the new RAF Harrier.

Rising costs and the small size of the proposed production run meant the British government dropped the idea of going it alone on a new-generation Harrier and opted to join the US AV-8B project. As well as the cost issues, the American composite wing had obvious weight advantages over the 'tin wing'. The new engine also offered enhanced performance. The clincher was that McDonnell Douglas were offering a far lower unit price than British industry could offer.

The newly privatised BAe and McDonnell

BELOW: The first production Harrier GR5s were delivered in 1985, but the type was quickly superseded by the night-attack GR7 variant.
Anthony Noble

Douglas joined forces to work on the AV-8B, with the British building the control system together with some aft fuselage sections, fins and carbon-fibre rudders and centreline stores pylons. In total, BAE received 40% work share on USMC and RAF aircraft, as well as 25% on export aircraft. The new aircraft was initially designated by the British as the Harrier GR5, with 96 being ordered by the RAF.

Once the project was underway, the RAF began proposing to fit British-specific elements including moving map displays, a defensive aid suite, identification friend or foe (IFF) and more stores pylons with UK-specific weapons integration. A British gun, the 25mm Royal Ordnance revolving cannon, was adopted by the RAF for installation in two under-fuselage pods.

The initial production Harrier GR5 were originally scheduled to be delivered in 1986, but the project suffered from a series of delays and the first aircraft were not handed over to the RAF for another year. A test pilot was killed in an accident because of a freak fault in the aircraft's ejector seat and it took several months to establish the cause. Then the Ferranti FIN 1075 inertial navigation system suffered problems during testing that needed to be fixed.

The first GR5 unit, 1 (Fighter) Squadron, was declared operational in 1988, but the aircraft were »

ABOVE: A Harrier GR7 lifts off from an Invincible-class aircraft carrier. MoD/Crown Copyright

LEFT: The Harrier GR7's nose contained a FLIR sensor and laser target tracker to accurately locate and attack targets at night. Tim Ripley

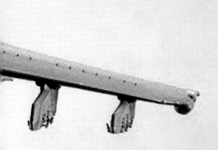

LEFT: Harrier GR7s used self-designated laser guided bombs for the first time during the 1999 Kosovo crisis. MoD/Crown Copyright

Designator (TIALD) targeting pod. Self-designating with a TIALD pod was only declared operational in 1998, just before the start of the war in Kosovo. GPS-guided Enhanced Paveway bombs were fielded ahead of the 2003 Iraq War.

The final iteration of the British Harrier was the GR9 variant that came into frontline use in 2007. It incorporated improved avionics, communications systems, and weapons capabilities, as well as replacing the composite rear fuselage to reduce fatigue. The GR9 featured an enhanced suite of weapons, including AGM-65 Maverick air-to-ground missiles, the Rangeless Airborne Instrumentation Debriefing System (RAIDS), Raytheon's Successor identification friend or foe (SIFF) system, Enhanced Paveway guided bombs, the Lockheed Martin Sniper advanced targeting pod and the Digital Joint Reconnaissance

LEFT: The British GR5/7/9 shared the distinctive larger wing developed by McDonnell Douglas for the AV-8B. BAE Systems

still not fully cleared to deliver all the required weapons. As the first production GR5s were rolling off the line at Dunsfold, the RAF started to show an interest in following the example of the US Marine Corps by modifying the GR5 for night operations by fitting a forward-looking infrared (FLIR) and making the cockpit night-vision goggle (NVG) compatible. This project was dubbed Nightbird and it eventually led to the fielding of the GR7 variant.

The GR7 took its maiden flight in November 1989 and the first aircraft were delivered to IV (Army Co-operation) Squadron in September 1990. Plans were developed to retrofit all the GR5s that had already been delivered to GR7 standard. The GR7 also started to be fitted with the Pegasus Mk105 engine to create the GR7A variant.

In July 1991, the entire GR5/7 fleet was grounded after three unexplained fires in their electrical wiring. The RAF refused to accept any more aircraft from BAe until the fault was identified and rectified. Eventually it was traced to chafing of wiring insulation and, after new wiring looms were designed and fitted, deliveries resumed.

Then fatigue cracks were discovered in the rear fuselage, requiring a fleet-wide repair. It took until 1992 for full clearances on the basic suite of GR7 weapons – iron bombs, cluster bombs and heatseeking air-to-air missiles – to be achieved but, even then, the aircraft did not have its own targeting pod to allow it designate targets for laser-guided bombs (LGBs).

Initial LGB capability was not achieved until the summer of 1995, but this involved 'buddy' lasing from a SEPECAT Jaguar equipped with a Thermal Imaging Airborne Laser

LEFT: RAF Harriers used the Joint Reconnaissance Pod to take digital aerial images of enemy targets and area of interest to allied intelligence. Tim Ripley

BELOW: The Ferranti TIALD was the first targeting pod to be integrated onto the Harrier. It was replaced by the US-made Sniper pod on GR9 aircraft for the Afghan campaign in 2007. Tim Ripley

Pod (DJRP). All these improvements were added during a combined maintenance/upgrade line at RAF Cottesmore, run by BAe Systems under the Joint Update and Maintenance Programme (JUMP).

The GR9 was considered 'the ultimate Harrier' and when they were withdrawn from service after the 2010 defence review, the USMC jumped at the chance to buy the surviving 72 aircraft for $116 million so they could harvest them for spare parts. There were suggestions that the USMC might reactivate them, but this never happened. It was a sad end to the British Harrier story.

BAE HARRIER GR7	
Length	14.12m (46ft 4in)
Wingspan	9.25m (30ft 4in)
Max take-off weight	14,061kg (31,000lb)
Maximum speed	1,065kph (662mph)
Combat range	560km (350miles)
Armament	Two 25 mm ADEN cannon pods, 38 CRV7 70 mm rockets in two pods, 4 or 6 AIM-9 Sidewinder air-to-air missiles, four AGM-65 Maverick missiles. Assorted bombs, including Paveway II/III/IV and Enhanced Paveway II/II+ laser-guided bombs, unguided 500lb and 1,000 lb bombs. Sniper and TIALD targeting pods.

TOP: After the introduction of the GR7 variant, RAF Harrier pilots could attack targets at night and in bad weather for the first time.
MoD/Crown Copyright

LEFT: The GR9 variant served in RAF and Fleet Air Arm Harrier units from 2007 until the retirement of the jump jet in 2010 as a result of Ministry of Defence spending cuts.
Adrian Pingstone

In October 2001, the Pentagon selected Lockheed Martin's solution for the joint strike fighter (JSF) programme, opening a new chapter in the jump jet story.

Work commenced to transition the X-35 prototype into aircraft that could go into production as the Lockheed Martin F-35 Lightning II. The USAF, US Navy and US Marine Corps were all participants in the F-35 programme, with 2,469 aircraft from three variants currently required.

The heart of the F-35 concept was to provide operators with a stealth or low observability aircraft that would be able to penetrate enemy air defences in any conflict. To reduce costs, all variants would share common avionics, mission systems

ABOVE: The X-32B prototype proved the aircraft's revolutionary lift fan worked as advertised.
Lockheed Martin

LEFT: The F-35B Lightning II is the only vertical take-off and landing fighter jet in production today.
MoD/Crown Copyright

F-35B LIGHTNING II

America's joint strike fighter goes vertical

and other electronics systems, as well as a common airframe design and engine.

The USAF was the biggest customer, with 1,763 conventional take-off and landing A-type variants on its shopping list. The US Navy and USMC wanted 273 and 140 'cat and trap' carrier-borne C-type variants, respectively. These had a slightly bigger wing to accommodate larger fuel tanks to extend range and an arrestor hook so they could be 'trapped' on aircraft carriers.

The final variant, the short take-off vertical landing (STOVL) B-type, was developed to meet the requirements of the USMC, with considerable input from the UK and Italy who were Tier 1 & 2 partners in the F-35 programme. They wanted the jet to replace their Harriers and Sea Harriers.

The F-35B was designed around the Pratt & Whitney F135-PW-60 engine and the unique Rolls-Royce lift fan, which required major modifications to be made to the airframe of the basic F-35. Just behind the cockpit was the lift fan, which was powered directly by the aircraft's engine via a shaft and gearbox. The vertical lift thrust was balanced by a rotating engine exhaust nozzle at the tail of

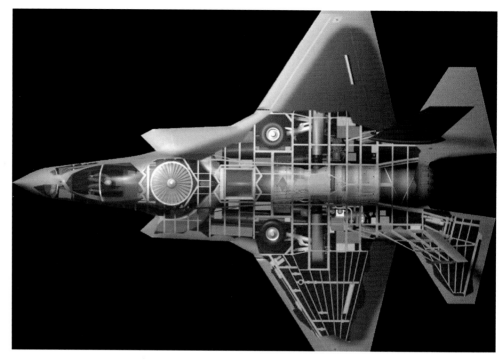

the aircraft and two small thrust nozzles embedded in the wings.

The F-35B's engine exhaust ran considerably hotter than the old Harrier, making it capable of burning concrete, tarmac, or steel ship decks if the aircraft landed or took off in pure vertical mode. To mitigate this, the USMC developed a

prefabricated heat-resistant landing pad. Ships that operated the F-35B had their flight decks coated with Thermion, an heat-resistant non-slip material. To enhance their weapon carrying capability, F-35Bs routinely used rolling take-offs and landings rather than vertical mode operations.

At the heart of the F-35 was its stealth features, which revolve around its fuselage and wing shape, using special radar absorbent coatings to reduce its radar cross-section to such an extent that the aircraft reputedly has the same radar return as a bird. The coatings are highly classified and need to be regularly touched-up by engineers to maintain their effectiveness.

The first F-35B flew in June 2008 and, once the design was proven, the initial aircraft was delivered to the USMC at VMFA-121 at Marine Corps Air Station Yuma in November 2012. Three years later, the squadron was declared fully operational as the world's first F-35B combat unit. Under current plans the USMC wants to stand up 12 F-35B active-duty squadrons and two fleet replenishment or operational conversion units.

The USMC uses its F-35Bs in a variety of roles to support its expeditionary operational concept. Small detachments of eight jets are embarked on amphibious ships as part of Marine Expeditionary Units (MEUs). Squadron-sized units operate from shore bases in support of large USMC brigades and divisions. As part of its experiments to counter Chinese threats in the Pacific region, the USMC has carried out exercises to rapidly »

ABOVE: The Rolls-Royce lift fan is installed in front of the F-35B's engine.
Lockheed Martin

LOCKHEED MARTIN F-35B LIGHTNING II	
Length	15.60m (51ft 2¼in)
Height	4.36m (14ft 3½in)
Wingspan	10.70m (35ft)
Maxi take-off weight	27,216kg (60,000lb)
Maxi speed	1,976kph (1,228mph)
Combat radius	on internal fuel 833km (450miles)
Armament	Typical, two AIM-9 or AIM-120 air-to-air missiles and two bombs carried internally, with optional underwing pylons enabling stores of up to 6,800kg (15,000lb)

LEFT: The F-35B's lift fan is powered directly by the aircraft's engine.
Duch Seb

move small contingents of F-35Bs to island airstrips or roads, with support equipment, fuel and weapons transferred by air in Boeing MV-22 Osprey tiltrotors.

Around 160 F-35Bs have been delivered to the USMC to date, out of a total requirement of 280 jets, but the ramp up of F-35B squadron was slowed by production problems with the TR-3/

Block upgrade in 2023-2024. This led to a year-long pause in deliveries to all customers and there is still uncertainty over the roll-out of many enhanced features to the aircraft.

While the USMC is the biggest customer of the F-35B, the variant is also selling well among former users of the Harrier. As the only in-production jump jet, the F-35B

is also proving to be popular with navies that are fielding new aircraft carriers over the coming decade.

Britain is the largest non-US F-35B customer, using them to provide embarked airpower on its two Queen Elizabeth-class aircraft carriers. By the end of 2024, 34 aircraft had been delivered out of an initial order for 48. An order for a second batch of 26 jets

LEFT: Britain's Queen Elizabeth-class carriers are fitted with ski jumps to help F-35Bs make rolling take-offs to enhance their performance, range, and endurance.
MoD/Crown Copyright

BELOW: The US Marine Corps has experimented with operating more than a dozen F-35Bs from US Navy amphibious assault ships.
US DoD/Combat Camera

LEFT: The US Marine Corps aims to have completed its transition to the F-35B from the AV-8B by 2027.
US DoD/Combat Camera

is being negotiated and Britain still has a target of 138 F-35Bs. As a Tier 1 partner in the JSF programme, the design of the F-35B incorporated many features required by the RAF and Royal Navy. The first test jets were delivered in 2012 and its first unit, 617 Squadron, was stood up in 2018.

Italy is currently the next biggest operator of the F-35Bs, for use on its new Cavour-class aircraft carrier, with 40 on order. In 2024, the ITS *Cavour* embarked F-35Bs for a long-range cruise to the Far East. Japan has 42 F-35Bs on order for its two Kaga-class amphibious ships, but production delays have hit the project, and no aircraft have been delivered yet. Spain has long been considered a prime target for the

F-35B to replace its AV-8B Harrier II Plus jets, but to date no order has been placed. South Korea is considering buying the F-35B for use on its Dokdo-class amphibious assault ships operated by the Republic of Korea Navy. Singapore has also expressed interest in F-35Bs for use from road strips or amphibious ships, with 12 aircraft on order, but deliveries have been delayed beyond 2026.

The F-35B looks like it will have a long future service life, with many users looking to operate it beyond 2050.

BELOW: F-35Bs routinely land back onboard ships using their lift fan to ease congestion on flight decks.
US DoD/Combat Camera

SUBSCRIBE TODAY!

FALKLAND ISLANDS 1982

Sea Harriers win air supremacy over the South Atlantic

ABOVE: HMS
Hermes was home
to the Sea Harrier
FRS1s of 800 Naval
Air Squadron
during the
Falklands conflict.
MoD/Crown Copyright

The battle for the Falklands in 1982 saw Royal Navy Sea Harrier FRS1s and RAF Harrier GR3s win their spurs in battle for the first time. Fleet Air Arm pilots took on Argentinian jets that were attacking the British task force in the San Carlos anchorage after May 21, inflicting heavy losses that broke the back of the enemy air offensive.

HMS *Hermes* and HMS *Invincible* sailed for the Falklands on April 5, 1982, with 20 Sea Harrier FRS1s from 800 and 801 Naval Air Squadrons (NAS) embarked. They were the key to the air defence of the British naval task force in the South Atlantic. The flamboyant commander of 801 NAS, Lieutenant Commander 'Sharky'

RIGHT: Sea
Harriers launched
from HMS
Hermes to bomb
the Falklands.
MoD/Crown Copyright

Ward, is now the stuff of legend after his pilots took on and defeated waves of Argentinian jets.

After an RAF Avro Vulcan bomber attacked Port Stanley airport in the early hours of May 1, the Sea Harriers joined the air offensive. "I'm not allowed to say how many planes joined the raid, but I counted them all out, and I counted them all back," was how veteran BBC correspondent Brian Hanrahan described the first Sea Harrier raid on Port Stanley. Ministry of Defence censors had refused to allow Hanrahan to give specific details about the raid.

The task group commander, Rear Admiral Sandy Woodward, positioned his aircraft carriers in striking range of Port Stanley at first light on May 1. The first two Harriers in the air took pictures of the damage caused by the Vulcan. Minutes after the recce jets made their pass, nine more Harriers roared across the airfield, dropping three 1,000lb bombs each. A fuel store was set on fire, and Argentine soldiers were forced to dive for cover. Anti-aircraft guns opened fire at the British jets, one of which took a round in its tail but was able to return safely to its carrier. The final

three Sea Harriers raided the grass airstrip at Goose Green, dropping cluster bombs over a pair of Pucara ground attack aircraft as they were preparing to take off, putting both out of action.

The Argentinian high command gave orders during the morning of May 1 to launch a major air and naval attack, but a dozen air force jets failed to locate any targets. This was the warm-up »

towards Port Stanley in the hope of making an emergency landing, only to be mistaken for a British jet and being shot down by friendly fire. A pair of Daggers were intercepted by Sea Harriers south of East Falkland, and one was hit by a Sidewinder as it tried to escape. Argentine commanders now pulled their jets back from the Falklands to await the main British amphibious landing, planned for May 21.

On the morning of the landing that put more than 5,000 British troops ashore, the Sea Harrier squadrons on HMS *Hermes* and HMS *Invincible* were mobilised for a maximum effort to keep the Argentine air force at bay. From first light, Sea Harriers flew combat air patrols (CAPs) to the north and south of Falkland Sound looking for attacking jets. Aerial combat over the Falklands that day pitted Argentinian and British pilots against each other in a deadly duel. They were flying 1960s and 1970s jets equipped with radars and guided missiles, but survival depended on split second reactions and keeping a constant eye on their fuel gauges.

Argentinian Mirages, Daggers and Skyhawks flying towards the Falklands always made the transit at ultra-low level to avoid British radar surveillance, then would try to hide behind the hills of West Falklands to give them the element of surprise on their final approach to the anchorage of the British »

LEFT: Sidewinder missiles and 1,000lb bombs being prepared for loading on the deck of HMS *Hermes*.
MoD/Crown Copyright

RIGHT: The Sea Harrier jump jet dominated the skies over the Falklands.
MoD/Crown Copyright

LEFT: Argentinian IAI Daggers were dispatched over the South Atlantic to strike back at the British.
Carlos Ay

BELOW: Port Stanley airport was hit by the first Sea Harrier air strike of the Falklands War on May 1, 1982, causing fires and damage across the hardened airport.
KES-6

act for a major Argentine air force strike in the afternoon. More than 50 jets, including 37 armed with bombs to hit ships, were launched simultaneously in a bid to swamp the British defences. One Canberra B.2 was shot down by a Sidewinder air-to-air missile from a Sea Harrier.

The Argentinian bombers were escorted by pairs of Mirage IIIEs and Daggers armed with air-to-air missiles, which flew at medium level so they could use their radars to look for Sea Harriers. Throughout the afternoon the rival fighters played a game of cat and mouse. A dogfight ensued to the north of Port Stanley, in which a pair of Mirages were jumped by two Sea Harriers, their Sidewinders finding their marks, destroying one Argentinian jet outright and damaging another. It limped

SEA HARRIERS IN THE FALKLANDS, 1982

Royal Navy – Fleet Air Arm
800 Naval Air Squadron
12 Sea Harrier FRS1s embarked on HMS *Hermes*
801 Naval Air Squadron
8 Sea Harrier FRS1s embarked on HMS *Invincible*
809 Naval Air Squadron
8 Sea Harrier FRS1s, four absorbed into 800 Squadron and four into 801 Squadron

patrol and had limited fuel, tested the pilots to the extreme. They could never relax until they were safely back on deck.

In the afternoon of May 21, the Sea Harrier patrols shot down their first Argentinian jets with heat-seeking Sidewinder AIM-9L missiles. By the end of the day, six kills were claimed. Over the next three days, five more aircraft were claimed by the Sea Harriers, all with Sidewinders.

May 25 marked the last time the Argentinian air force managed to launch an attack on the British anchorage in San Carlos. The back of the Argentine air assault was broken. From now on, the presence of Sea Harrier patrols was enough to force the Argentinian pilots to turn for home without even pressing home their attacks on the anchorage.

LEFT: A Sea Harrier diverted to land on HMS *Fearless* to refuel after a helicopter accident temporarily put the San Carlos forward operating strip out of action. MoD/Crown Copyright

BELOW: Eight Sea Harriers were carried to the South Atlantic onboard the converted container ship, SS *Atlantic Conveyor*. MoD/Crown Copyright

amphibious shipping in San Carlos Water and Falkland Sound. After popping up over the final mountain range on West Falklands, the Argentine pilots had a matter of seconds to scan the water below for British ships and pick a target. This was the moment when British anti-aircraft shells and missiles started to come towards them.

Even after pulling up from the attack runs, the danger was not over for the Argentinian pilots. Positioned around the anchorage were Sea Harrier combat air patrols, which swooped down to try to engage the jets as they attempted to escape. With their fuel state at critical, there was no ability to turn and fight their pursuers. Their only option was to try to go low, merge with the hills and islands and hope they could outrun the Sea Harriers.

Sea Harrier pilots had to make split-second decisions on whether to engage their enemies. Fortunately, the Argentinian jets rarely turned on their pursuers. There were often just too many enemy aircraft and no time to identify the most important targets. Once committed to engaging a jet, the British pilots had to dive to get on their tail, then close to get missile lock. Keeping a fast-moving jet in their sights, often at low level, for a vital few minutes was an extreme test of the British pilots' skills.

Just like their adversaries, the Sea Harrier pilots were flying at the edge of their endurance envelope. They had to keep a constant eye on their fuel state and be ready to break off their combat air patrols to return to HMS *Hermes* or HMS *Invincible*. The extreme weather in the South Atlantic could change with little notice, so returning to their carrier when they were tired after a long

LEFT: HMS *Invincible* remained on station in the South Atlantic during the summer of 1982 to protect the islands until the RAF air defence fighters were firmly established in Port Stanley.
MoD/Crown Copyright

During the last two weeks of the conflict, the Sea Harriers tightened their grip on airspace around the Falklands, shooting down a Hercules transporter and Canberra bomber. Three Dagger jets were destroyed during a major raid on June 8 against British landing ships operating south of Port Stanley.

The Sea Harriers from HMS *Hermes* and HMS *Invincible* inflicted serious losses on the Argentine Air Force, destroying 23 aircraft in air-to-air engagements, for the loss of not a single Sea Harrier. Six Sea Harriers were lost in Operation Corporate, including two shot down and four in accidents. Four Sea Harrier pilots were killed in action.

BELOW: The turbulent waters of the South Atlantic were the backdrop to Sea Harrier operations in the Falklands.
MoD/Crown Copyright

FALKLAND ISLANDS 1982

GR3 ground attack operations

four more RAF jets made the seven-hour non-stop flight from Ascension Island to HMS *Hermes,* with the help of air-to-air refuelling from Handley Page Victor tankers.

The RAF Harrier pilots barely had time to rest before they took to the skies to strike Argentinian targets in the run up to the British landing at San Carlos on May 21. Three Argentinian helicopters were damaged by a cluster bomb and cannon attack on May 20.

The GR3s made a decisive intervention during a major attack by British paratroopers to capture Goose Green from a strong Argentinian garrison, despite a Harrier being shot down on May 27. The following day, as the British were bogged down by Argentine troops, Harriers were called in to cluster bomb their positions. The Argentines surrendered a few hours later.

British engineers built an improvised airstrip for Harriers at San Carlos, complete with fuel dumps and metal ramps to park the aircraft while they waited to be called into action. This meant the GR3s could stand strip alert ashore, ready to be called forward to attack the Argentine forces preparing

A s the Royal Navy's Sea Harrier FRS1s were winning the battle for air supremacy against Argentina, the RAF was building up its strike force onboard HMS *Hermes* by dispatching ten Harrier GR3 ground attack aircraft to the South Atlantic.

The RAF had initially mobilised 1 (Fighter) Squadron from RAF Wittering to back up losses among the Sea Harriers, but by the time the first GR3 landed on HMS *Hermes* on May 18, 1982, the situation had shifted. The RAF jets were earmarked for ground attack missions, freeing Sea Harriers to concentrate on defending the fleet.

Getting the RAF Harriers to the South Atlantic was not easy. The first six GR3s were embarked on a converted container ship, the SS *Atlantic Conveyor,* and once the ship arrived in the South Atlantic, they lifted off from an improvised flight deck to make the hop to HMS *Hermes* from May 18. In the first week of June,

for their last stand at Port Stanley. Both the Sea Harriers and GR3s were able to use the airstrip. Aircraft flew in from the fleet at first light and stayed on task until nightfall, saving fuel and allowing the two British carriers to remain safely out of range of Argentine air attacks.

The 1 (F) Squadron jets were provided with laser-guided bombs (LGBs) to carry out pinpoint attacks on troop positions. After several belated attempts to use the bombs, an RAF Harrier managed to use one against an Argentine artillery battery on June 13, just hours before Argentina surrendered.

The deployment of 1 (F) Squadron to the South Atlantic was the first time RAF aircraft had operated from Royal Navy ships since World War Two. Theys made a decisive contribution to the British victory, including using LGBs in combat for the first time. This was not without costs. Four RAF Harriers were lost, including three shot down and one written off after suffering engine failure when attempting to land at San Carlos. No RAF Harrier pilots were killed, but one was captured, becoming the only British pilot to be taken prisoner during the conflict.

USMC Harriers headed to Saudi Arabia in August 1990, refuelling from USAF KC-10 tankers over the Atlantic and Mediterranean.
US DoD/Combat Camera

Capt N.E Alberts (Fats), XO-Maj R.C. Branch(stur

I n response to the Iraqi invasion of the Gulf state of Kuwait in August 1990, US President George HW Bush ordered more than 100,000 American troops to head to the Middle East to stop further Iraqi advances.

The United States Marine Corps (USMC) was in the forefront of this response and the first 'Leathernecks' of the 7th Marine Expeditionary Brigade touched down in Saudia Arabia on August 14, 1990, less than two weeks after the Iraqi invasion. This was the first wave of the build-up of the 1 Marine Expeditionary Force (1MEF) that would eventually amount to 85,000 personnel by February 1991. This military force included more than 220 fixed wing aircraft and 170 helicopters under the command of the 3rd Marine Air Wing (3 MAW), based in Saudi Arabia, Bahrain or on ships in the northern Arabian Gulf.

USMC leaders in the Gulf were keen to use the airpower under their command to minimise US casualties and speed up the expulsion of Iraqi leader Saddam Hussein's troops from Kuwait.

Just as the first US Marines were landing at Dhahran Air Base in Saudi Arabia, a USMC McDonnell Douglas AV-8B Harrier II squadron was touching down at Sheik Isa Air Base in Bahrain, after flying across the Atlantic. After a few days on the ground, they relocated to King Abdul Aziz Airfield, outside the port of Al Jubail, to stand ready to provide close

OPERATION DESERT
STORM 1991

USMC Harrier operations liberate Kuwait

USMC Harrier pilots pressed home their attacks on Iraqi tank columns and artillery batteries in the face to barrages of surface-to-air missiles and anti-aircraft artillery fire. Corporal LCOZLL, USMC

Frank D. Smith (pugs), & Capt. D. Peros(Machine)

USMC AV-8B SQUADRONS OPERATION DESERT STORM 1991

King Abdul Aziz Airfield, Kingdom of Saudi Arabia
• VMA-311 (20 x AV-8B)
• VMA-542 (20 x AV-8B)
• VMA-231 (20 x AV-8B)

USS *Nassau*, Arabian Gulf
• VMA-331 (20 x AV-8B)

USS *Tarawa*, Arabian Gulf
• VMA-513 Detachment B (6 x AV-8B)

A third AV-8B unit, VMA-331, arrived in the Gulf aboard the USS *Nassau* as a floating reserve. Once all the amphibious vessel's marines had disembarked, the ship was converted into the first 'Harrier carrier' to conduct strike missions. In November 1990, President Bush ordered a second wave of reinforcement to the Gulf to allow US-led coalition forces to take the offensive to eject the Iraqis from Kuwait. This saw two more AV-8B units, VMA 231 and Det B of VMA 513, arrived at King Abdul Aziz Airfield to bring the number of Harriers ashore to 66. A further 20 AV-8Bs were embarked on the USS *Nassau*.

USMC Harrier pilots were in the air a few hours after Operation »

BOTTOM: Harriers from VMA-331 operated from the USS *Nassau* during Operation Desert Storm, proving the 'Harrier carrier' concept. US DoD/Combat Camera

BELOW: The AV-8B made its combat debut in Operation Desert Storm and lived up to the expectations of USMC commanders who had backed buying the Harriers. US DoD/Combat Camera

air support to US Marine combat units along the Saudi-Kuwait border, 300 miles to the north. Within hours of the 20 jets of VMA-311 arriving at the disused oil industry airstrip, four had been turned around, refuelled, and put on 24/7 alert.

The crews of VMA-311 took over a part-built sports stadium next to the airstrip as their administrative site. US Navy and USMC engineers then set to work turning the airstrip into a fully functioning airbase. There were few luxuries for the squadron's personnel as they kept their jets at peak readiness in the oppressive summer heat. A few weeks later, US Navy cargo ships arrived at Jubail port with more maintenance equipment, spare parts and building supplies to speed up the work. More importantly, the ships started to unload huge quantities of bombs to allow the Harriers to potentially sustain strikes on the Iraqi army for several months. This allowed a second AV-8B squadron, VMA-542, to take up residence alongside VMA-311. Marine Air Group 13 (Forward) command staff arrived to take charge of the expanding air base.

Work then started on a forward arming and refuelling point (FARP) at Tanajib, less than 80 miles from the Kuwait border, to allow the Harriers to sustain intensive air operations nearer to the battlefield. This was another former oil industry airfield with minimal facilities. Its runway was too short for other fast jets, but the USMC Harriers did not find it a problem.

ABOVE: Harriers routinely returned to base with empty bomb racks during Operation Desert Storm.
US DoD/Combat Camera

BELOW: 'Dumb' or 'iron' bombs were the main ordnance used by AV-8Bs during Operation Desert Storm, but the jet targeting system ensured pilots could drop their weapons with a high degree of accuracy.
US DoD/Combat Camera

Desert Storm began on January 17, 1991, striking Iraqi artillery batteries that were firing on coalition troop positions inside Saudi Arabia. Under the coalition warplan, 1MEF was assigned to advance directly across the Saudi border and drive north to liberate Kuwait City, while the main US Army force was to drive deep into Iraq to cut off the retreat of Saddam Hussein's troops. A huge air offensive was to pummel the Iraqi army units in Kuwait until they were below 50% strength, opening the way for 1MEF to rapidly advance.

As the coalition air offensive escalated, the USMC AV-8Bs settled into a battle rhythm. Kuwait was divided into a series of 'kill-boxes', which were patrolled by airborne forward air control (AFAC) jets, which searched for targets to attack. AFAC Rockwell OV-10 Bronco and McDonnell Douglas F/A-18D Hornet aircraft of 3 MAW were assigned to patrol Kuwait in advance of the wing's strike jets.

The AFAC's were airborne throughout daylight hours looking for any Iraqi tanks or artillery batteries. A non-stop stream of Harriers was sent over Kuwait each day, so they were on hand to rapidly strike at targets found by the AFACs. Other jets were held on strip alert at Tanajib,

ready to scramble to attack enemy targets.

The austere Tanajib airfield was the key to sustaining the tempo of AV-8B missions over Kuwait. Once the jets had expended all their ordnance, they would land at Tanajib to refuel and re-arm, before heading back into the fight. Jets were on the ground for less than an hour. The AFACs and Harrier pilots established a slick working relationship and got to know the battle situation very well, allowing them to put bombs on target in a matter of minutes of them being located.

Weather conditions over Kuwait in January and February were poor, with low cloud, rain and sandstorms being common. This meant the Harrier pilots often had to dive below 8,000ft on their bomb runs, leaving them vulnerable to Iraqi heat-seeking shoulder-launched surface-to-air missiles. Five Harriers were lost in the Gulf War, with two pilots killed, two captured and one recovered safely by coalition troops.

The 86 USMC AV-8Bs amassed 3,380 flights and about 4,100 flight hours during Desert Storm, with a mission availability rate of more than 90%. The Harriers achieved impressive kill rates against Iraqi targets but, more importantly, USMC commanders were impressed by the ability of the AV-8B squadrons to keep a near non-stop flow of jets over the battlefield. The Harriers were considered a key asset in the success of 1MEF. No other fixed wing jet was able

RIGHT: When USMC columns entered Kuwait, they found thousands of tanks and other military vehicles that had been devastated by coalition air strikes, including 3,000 attack missions by USMC AV-8Bs. US DoD/ Combat Camera

to operate so intensely over the Kuwait battlefield.

The investment by the USMC in the Harrier fleet over the previous 20 years was paid back in spades during the Gulf War. For Desert Storm, 1MEF suffered only 24 killed in action and 92 wounded, which USMC senior commanders largely attributed to the superlative air support they received from 3 MAW and its Harrier squadrons.

RIGHT: US Navy amphibious ships staged Harrier strikes off the coast of Kuwait during Operation Desert Storm to divert Iraqi troops to coastal defence duties. US DoD/ Combat Camera

BOSNIA AND IRAQ NO-FLY ZONES

Aerial peacekeeping in the 1990s

ABOVE: The upgraded Harrier GR7 was at the forefront of the RAF's contribution to NATO's first major bombing campaign in Bosnia. Jeremy Flack

Bosnia

After the former Yugoslavia descended into civil war in 1992, Britain joined the United Nations and NATO peacekeeping operations in the Balkan country in a bid to contain fighting and stop atrocities against the civilian population.

British air power became actively involved in protecting UN-declared 'safe areas' in Bosnia in 1993, when RAF SEPECAT Jaguars started flying patrols from Gioia del Colle Air Base in southern Italy to deter attacks on UN peacekeepers. The Jaguar pilots patrolling Bosnia were handicapped by a lack of precision guided weapons and, on several occasions, struggled to find camouflaged Serb tanks and artillery in poor visibility. This prompted a major rethink of RAF laser-guided bombing policy, and an urgent operation requirement programme was launched to fit the 12 Jaguars with TIALD targeting pods

RIGHT: Bosnian Serb ammunition bunkers near Sarajevo were among the first targets attacked by RAF Harrier GR5s during Operation Deliberate Force. Nato/Afsouth

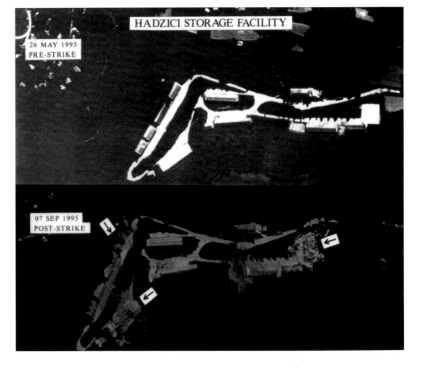

HADZICI STORAGE FACILITY

26 MAY 1995 PRE-STRIKE

07 SEP 1995 POST-STRIKE

to allow them to direct laser-guided bombs (LGBs) during missions in Bosnia.

The Fleet Air Arm was called into action over Bosnia for the first time in April 1994, when British troops trapped in the besieged city of Gorazde came under attack. Two 801 Naval Air Squadron Sea Harrier FRS1s launched from HMS *Ark Royal* to attack Serb positions, but as they rolled in to drop their bombs, one was shot down by a Serb heat-seeking missile. The pilot safely ejected and was recovered by British troops.

The Jaguar squadrons were due to hand over the Bosnia commitment to the Harrier force in the summer of 1995, but the need to give the jump jets a precision-guided strike capability remained. So, a handful of Jaguar crews started working with the BAe Harriers GR7s of IV (Air Co-operation) Squadron to train them up to drop LGBs, directed by the TIALD-equipped Jaguars. A pair of Jaguars were kept on alert at RAF Coltishall, ready to fly to Italy

if a major operation requiring the Harriers to drop LGBs was required.

The trigger for the unleashing of NATO airpower was a random mortar attack on Sarajevo on the morning of August 28, 1995, that left 37 civilians dead and scores wounded. Within hours, NATO and the UN had completed preparations for a series of air strikes that would dramatically alter the military balance in Bosnia.

It was quickly determined that the Serbs were the culprits behind the mortar attack and that a major air response would be executed. After the UN commander, Lieutenant General Rupert Smith, ordered the small British garrison in Gorazde to make a dash for safety in Yugoslavia, he turned the UN bombing key, while US Navy Admiral Snuffy Smith did the same for the NATO key. The clock was now ticking towards the launch of Operation Deliberate Force.

To bolster the capabilities of the IV (AC) Squadron's Harrier GR7 contingent in Italy, a pair of 6

Squadron's Jaguar GR1B fitted with TIALD pods were scrambled to guide the Harrier's bombs. NATO aircraft started taking off late in the evening of August 29, bound for targets in eastern Bosnia. The RAF joined the offensive later that day as NATO dispatched a stream of strike packages over the country to systematically degrade the Bosnian Serbs' military capabilities.

A typical package would include two British Harriers and a Jaguar GR1B, two or four American Lockheed F-16C Fighting Falcons, four US Navy McDonnell Douglas F/A-18C Hornets and two Dutch F-16As, which would work over the targets with LGBs. Following behind would be a pair of reconnaissance aircraft to photograph the results of each raid, former of either British Harriers, French Dassault Mirage F.1CRs, Dutch F-16A(R)s or US Navy Grumman F-14A Tomcats. The packages usually either attacked a single target complex, such as an ammunition dump, or would go »

after different aim points around Sarajevo and elsewhere in eastern Bosnia. NATO steadily escalated pressure by hitting more and more targets in north and western Bosnia.

On September 9, UN troops near Tuzla came under Serb fire and called on NATO for close air support to neutralise the threat. After US and Dutch jets dropped bombs on the artillery battery, a pair of RAF Harrier GR7s, which had been flying a photographic reconnaissance mission, were told to stop what they were doing and help the UN troops. The Harriers were to employ their laser target spotting devices for the first time.

These picked up a laser beam bounced off the target by a UN forward air controller's laser designator, then automatically programmed the aircraft's attack system to release its 1,000lb 'iron' bomb along an appropriate trajectory to hit the target. The first Harrier pilot had a problem setting his bomb fuse for an air burst and aborted, but the second aircraft's system worked perfectly.

Later in the day, French Jaguars, RAF Harriers, and RAF Jaguars carried out a decisive LGB strike on a key telecommunications mast north of Tuzla. The British and French aircraft toppled the mast

and knocked out a key Bosnian Serb Army communications link just as Croat troops were launching an offensive against the Serbian stronghold of Banja Luka in western Bosnia. Video footage showed one of the towers falling to the earth after a laser guided bomb ripped into its foundations.

Three days later, the NATO bombing offensive finally brought the Serb leadership to the table. After US negotiators met Yugoslav leader Slobodan Milosevic in Belgrade, Sarajevo airport and road routes into the Bosnian capital were reopened on September 14. A few weeks later,

a nationwide ceasefire was declared, opening the way for the Dayton Peace Accords, which formally ended the war on December 20, 1995.

The RAF flew 326 sorties during Operation Deliberate Force, some 9% of the NATO total, delivering 48 LGBs and 32 1,000lb 'iron' bombs. The Harrier detachment alone flew 144 sorties. Operation Deliberate Force was the RAF's first major operation in which precision-guided munitions predominated.

Iraq

In the aftermath of the 1991 Gulf War, the US, Britain, and other allies launched air and land operations to protect Kurdish refugees who had fled to mountainous regions along the Iraqi-Turkish border to escape an offensive by Saddam Hussein's troops. The mission was to safeguard the Kurds and allow them to return home under the protection of allied troops. To prevent a repeat of the exodus, the allies set up a no-fly zone over the Kurdish enclave patrolled by aircraft based at Incirlik airbase in Turkey.

A contingent of eight RAF Jaguars arrived at Incirlik in September 1991 and remained on duty for two years, when three RAF Harrier units replaced them. Operation Warden involved a package of allied aircraft making a daily foray over northern Iraq to demonstrate resolve and show the Iraqi air defences that the allies were still around. A pair of Harriers were usually tasked to join the package,

with the mission of photographing Iraqi positions so that allied commanders could assess if Saddam Hussein's troops were threatening the Kurdish enclave.

During the first four months of 1998, RAF Harrier GR7s and Fleet

Air Arm Sea Harrier FA2s joined Operation Bolton patrolling the no-fly zone over southern Iraq from a Royal Navy aircraft carrier in the Northern Arabian Gulf. HMS *Invincible* and then HMS *Illustrious* provided this duty.

BELOW: A 1 (F) Squadron Harrier GR7 lands on HMS *Illustrious*.
MoD/Crown Copyright

KOSOVO 1999

Operation Allied Force challenges Serbia

VEVIVOLO ARMATO PERICOLO ⚠ AIRCRAFT ARMED DANGER

ABOVE: Harrier GR7s were kept on ground alert at Gioia del Colle Air Base in Italy to scramble if targets were identified by allied air reconnaissance.
MoD/Crown Copyright

had trained for. Along with two other Harrier squadrons, they were the RAF's specialist close air support and battlefield air interdiction units. The first Harrier had deployed to Gioia del Colle in Italy in October 1998 as NATO had started to ramp up its preparations for war.

In February 1999, 1 (F) Squadron arrived with eight Harriers to take its turn on duty and found itself in the forefront of Operation Allied Force until June, when the Serbs agreed to pull back. For the first time, the Harriers were equipped with their own TIALD targeting pods, thus could self-designate their own laser-guided bombs (LGBs) and not have to rely on Jaguars to do it for them.

To destroy the Serb army in Kosovo, NATO air commanders in the Combined Air Operations Centre (CAOC) in Italy had to create from scratch a system for finding and locating targets on a fast-moving and

NATO intervention in Bosnia after 1995 largely stabilised the Balkan country, but three years later the Yugoslav province of Kosovo was engulfed in more violence after Serbian forces tried to contain unrest by its majority Albanian population. International diplomacy failed to resolve the crisis, so on March 24, 1999, NATO launched an air operation to try to bring the Yugoslavian leader Slobodan Milosevic to the negotiating table.

NATO jets, including RAF BAe Harrier GR7s, were sent to hit ammunition dumps and communication towers around the capital of Kosovo, Pristina. The first wave of US strategic strikes also attacked targets across Yugoslavia.

Once dawn rose, it became clear that the Yugoslav military had not been crippled by the attacks. Milosevic appeared defiant and his paramilitary police started evicting thousands of Albanian civilians from their homes in Pristina and dumping them at crossing points on the borders with Albania and Macedonia. Within days, tens of thousands of refugees were fleeing Kosovo, at which point destroying the Yugoslav army in Kosovo became the priority of NATO air power.

This was the job the RAF Harrier GR7 pilots of 1 (Fighter) Squadron

RIGHT: The intensity of the operations by 1 (Fighter) Squadron's Harrier GR7s are indicated by these bomb markings. Tim Ripley

PRISTINA EXPLOSIVES STORAGE FACILITY, SERBIA

PRE STRIKE **POST STRIKE**

ABOVE: Serb targets across Kosovo were hit by RAF Harriers in the opening hours of Operation Allied Force. US DoD/ Combat Camera

BELOW: RAF Harrier GR7s deployed to Gioia del Colle Air Base in Italy in 1998 as part of the build-up to war. Tim Ripley

chaotic battlefield. This was a classic air interdiction effort and the time-proven tactic of using 'kill boxes', was used again. Kosovo was divided up into a series of 'engagement zones', as they had to be called for public relations reasons, and each was assigned an Airborne Forward Air Control (AFAC) aircraft. Once the attack aircraft were over the target, it was the AFAC's job to mark them with white phosphorous rockets or 500lb bombs to allow the 'bomb droppers' to hit their targets on their first run.

This system was designed to give the interdiction effort a dynamic element, to allow NATO to react quickly to sudden movements by the Serb army. However, it proved to be a slow business. On top of this, political concerns about civilian casualties meant very tight rules of engagement were put in place. While tanks in the open were fair game for NATO pilots, any targets in populated areas or near refugee columns could not be engaged without approval from the CAOC. It had to verify the pilot's initial report by other means, such as

other NATO pilots, unmanned aerial vehicles (UAVs) or signals intelligence reports. Not surprisingly this proved to be a time-consuming process and often meant NATO jets had to break off their attacks to refuel from tankers, while waiting for the CAOC to clear them, giving the Serbs time to disappear under cover again.

At the height of the air offensive, one RAF Harrier pilot said that finding good targets was far from easy. He called Kosovo a 'dead country' of burning but deserted villages: "It looked just like Bosnia during that war. There was nothing moving around at all during the daytime." »

much use as they would have wanted of their new TIALD pods to carry out precision strikes with LGBs. With cloud cover making it hard to identify targets, the Harriers had to revert to using old-fashioned BL755 cluster bombs to strike at Serb tanks and artillery positions with limited effectiveness.

The convoluted rules of engagement for identifying and hitting targets often meant the Harriers started to reach critical fuel levels – 'bingo fuel' in pilot jargon – and pull off their attack runs to refuel from one of the RAF Lockheed Tristar tankers orbiting outside Kosovo airspace. The number of Harriers was also ramped up from eight at the start of the campaign, with four more deployed at the end of March and another four sent to Italy at the beginning of May.

Operation Allied Force continued into April and May, with the campaign turning into a war of attrition. The 1 (F) Squadron pilots recounted that there was never an obvious tipping point in the conflict, just a daily grind of mission after mission. By the time the Serbs agreed to pull their troops out of Kosovo in June 1999, 1 (F) Squadron had flown more than 850 sorties. Its pilots had faced heavy enemy anti-aircraft fire and had to try to find targets in depths of the Balkan winter. Fortunately, no Harriers were lost in action.

There was satisfaction among the RAF Harrier crews that they had played a part in an ultimately successful air campaign but claims by senior NATO officers that the Yugoslav army had lost hundreds of tanks to air strikes proved illusory. The RAF had lots of precision-guided munitions and targeting pods, but its fast jet pilots and reconnaissance systems could not see through cloud or inside underground car parks. Better weapons and sensors were needed.

The Serb army had simply gone to ground in Kosovo, hiding in forests, villages, factories, and towns to keep out of sight of NATO surveillance. The Harrier pilot observed: "When General Clark got up and said knocking out five tanks was a good day for NATO, he was telling it straight. On some days we couldn't find any tanks. We never saw a really large group of targets. It would have been nice to get a good target to hit."

"Half the trouble was the weather," said another frustrated RAF pilot. "We needed to start ignoring collateral [damage] and start smashing targets, but the politicians [were] not ready to do that."

The poor weather conditions meant the Harrier pilots could not make as

KOSOVO 1999

Italian and USMC AV-8Bs strike from the sea

ABOVE: The air campaign to force the withdrawal of Serbian troops from Kosovo in 1999 was supported by USMC AV-8Bs from USS *Nassau* and USS *Kearsage.*
US DoD/Combat Camera

USMC AV-8B Harrier IIs of VMA-231 and VMA-542 saw action during the Kosovo conflict in 1999, flying from the amphibious ships in the Adriatic. Once Operation Allied Force commenced in March 1999, the 24th Marine Expeditionary Unit stood alert in the USS *Nassau* to rescue downed NATO air crew. The Harriers of VMA-542 then began to be integrated into allied strike packages operating over Kosovo after April 14.

At the end of April 1999, USS *Nassau* was relieved by USS *Kearsage*, with eight VMA-231 Harriers embarked. VMA-231's AV-8B pilots were no strangers to the Balkans, having deployed to the region in the summer of 1995 to stand alert to support combat search and rescue missions to recover US and allied pilots who had been shot down and flew 'top cover' during the June 1995 mission to rescue USAF F-16 pilot Scott O'Grady. One of the squadron's Harrier was lost over the Adriatic due to a mechanical problem on May 2, 1999, but the pilot was safely recovered.

In 1995, ITS *Giuseppe Garibaldi* had sailed to Somalia for her first combat cruise to provide air support for UN peacekeeping troops as they withdrew from the country. Her AV-8B Plus Harriers flew more than 100 missions but did not drop any bombs in anger. It was not until 1999 that the ship's AV-8Bs got their combat debut in Kosovo, flying in support of the NATO air campaign. This was also the first combat employment of carrier aviation by the Italian Marina Militare. Between May and June 1999, *Giuseppe Garibaldi*'s Harriers flew 30 combat sorties, dropping laser-guided bombs and firing Maverick air-to-ground missiles.

AFGHANISTAN 2001

USMC AV-8Bs assist boots on the ground

Peleliu and USS *Bataan* in a wave of helicopters on November 26 and captured Forward Operating Base Rhino in what turned out to be an unopposed assault. Once American troops were on the ground' in Afghanistan, the Taliban started to mobilise attacks against Rhino. At this point, the two AV-8B squadrons stepped up their patrols around the desert outpost, striking convoys of armed

After the terrorist attacks on the World Trade Center and Pentagon on September 11, 2001, US President George W Bush ordered a massive military response to destroy al-Qaeda leader Osama bin Laden's network of bases in Afghanistan.

US air and missile strikes opened Operation Enduring Freedom on October 7, 2001, to prepare for the day when the US would send troops to clear and capture al-Qaeda bases. Central Intelligence Agency (CIA) operatives and US Army Special Forces troops were on the ground as the air offensive began, working with local tribes that were hostile to al-Qaeda and their protectors in the Taliban regime that controlled Afghanistan.

Off the coast of Pakistan, the USS *Peleliu* and its amphibious group were poised to launch the embarked US Marines to seize the first foothold in Afghanistan. To support the 15th

Marine Expeditionary Unit (MEU) was the detachment of six AV-8B Harrier IIs from VMA-311. They did not immediately join the US-led air offensives, but held back to provide combat search and rescue coverage should any of the USAF heavy bombers and US Navy carrier-borne aircraft go down over enemy territory. In November 2001, this changed and VMA-311's jets started flying bombing missions from the USS *Peleliu,* using air-to-air refuelling from RAF Vickers VC10 and Lockheed Tristar tanker aircraft, striking targets identified by US air controllers and tribes fighting the Taliban.

In the build-up to a helicopter-borne operation to seize a disused airfield outside Kandahar in southwestern Afghanistan, USS *Peleliu* was joined by the USS *Bataan*, with another MEU and six more AV-8Bs of VMA-223 embarked.

On November 26, the US Marines of Task Force 58 took off from USS

BELOW: USMC Harriers from the USS *Peleliu* struck at targets in Afghanistan in the opening weeks of Operation Enduring Freedom in November 2001.
US DoD/Combat Camera

Taliban pick-up trucks with bombs or strafing runs.

Taliban resistance didn't last long and soon Task Force 58 was spreading out across Afghanistan to link up with allied tribes. Further reinforcements arrived, including the eight Italian AV-8Bs embarked on ITS *Giuseppe Garibaldi*. They joined forces with USMC counterparts to fly security patrols. In two months of operations, the Italian Harriers flew 288 sorties.

During December 2001, the USS *Peleliu* turned for home and her place was taken by the USS *Bonhomme Richard* with six Harriers of VMA-211 embarked. The USS *Bataan* departed in January 2002. The VMA-211 Harriers were thrown into battle to

help US airborne troops ambushed by al-Qaeda fighters during Operation Anaconda in March 2002. After an intense period of combat, the *Bonhomme Richard* left to be replaced by USS *Wasp*. Her six Harriers of VMA-542 were the first AV-8Bs to deploy to an operational theatre fitted with the second-generation Litening II targeting pod.

USS *Wasp* spent five months on station, but the Harriers had little to do as the Taliban and al-Qaeda were effectively scattered and unable to put up serious resistance. In October 2002, six AV-8Bs of VMA-513 were dispatched to Bagram Air Base in central Afghanistan to provide air support for US and NATO

peacekeeping troops deployed in small detachments around the country. During its 11 month stay, it flew 1,250 combat sorties and dropped 17 laser-guided bombs, two 5in Zuni rockets and 1,922 25mm cannon rounds. Afghanistan was now largely peaceful and the squadron was not replaced.

The opening months of Operation Enduring Freedom saw the USMC Harriers in the thick of the action, but AV-8Bs were not deployed in large numbers. Except for VMA-513, they were kept embarked on ships and used air-to-air refuelling to reach Afghanistan, so the AV-8Bs never really put their short take-off and landing capabilities to use.

BELOW: An AV-8B pilot checks his bombs on the USS *Peleliu* before heading over Afghanistan in support of Task Force 58.
US DoD/Combat Camera

OPERATION IRAQI FREEDOM 2003

AV-8Bs support the drive to Baghdad

ABOVE: The USS *Nassau* was home to Harriers of VMU-231 during Operation Iraqi Freedom in March and April 2003.
US DoD/Combat Camera

In January 2003, the USMC AV-8B Harrier II squadrons found themselves heading back to the Middle East for another showdown with Iraq.

Operation Iraqi Freedom was a full-on invasion to overthrow Saddam Hussein and his authoritarian regime, with more than 400,000 US troops, including 74,000 US Marines, deployed to the Middle East to lead the advance on Baghdad.

The USMC contributed I Marine Expeditionary Force (I MEF) to the invasion force and it started gathering in Kuwait during the first two months of 2003. The 3rd Marine Air Wing (3 MAW) provided air support, and it concentrated its fixed wing jets at Ahmed Al Jaber Air Base in Kuwait. The US air commanders were struggling to find air bases for all the hundreds of jets taking part in the invasion. Ramp space was at a premium at every air base, so 3 MAW commanders came up with an innovative solution to get their Harriers into the fight: converting two amphibious assault ships into 'Harrier Carriers', each embarking 24 AV-8B Harrier IIs. A dozen more jets from two other squadrons were embarked on two other US Navy assault ships. A further AV-8B

RIGHT: Satellite-guided JDAM bombs about to be loaded on USMC AV-8Bs at Ahmed Al Jaber Air Base in Kuwait in April 2003.
Tim Ripley

squadron was sent ashore to Ahmed Al Jaber, which was established as a super forward arming and refuelling point (FARP) to support the shipborne jets.

The AV-8Bs taking part in Operation Iraqi Freedom had been improved considerably since Operation Desert Storm in 1991. The most significant enhancement was the fitting of Litening II targeting pods, designed by the Israeli company Rafael. This third-generation pod had a high-definition thermal imaging camera that allowed the pilot to see even small targets at night or in bad weather. The USMC also dispatched an experimental system to the Middle East that allowed video imagery from Litening IIs to be downloaded and viewed live on a laptop computer used by forward air controllers on the ground. This dramatically speeded up the identification of targets, so the Harrier

RIGHT: For operations deep in Iraq, USMC AV-8Bs could call on the services of USAF and RAF tanker air-to-air refuelling tankers.
US DoD/Combat Camera

BOTTOM: To find targets in congested urban battlefields, USMC AV-8Bs were equipped with Litening II targeting pods.
Tim Ripley

USMC AV-8B SQUADRONS IN OPERATION IRAQI FREEDOM 2003

Ahmed Al Jaber Air Base, Kuwait
• VMA-214 (16 x AV-8B)

USS *Bonhomme Richard*, Arabian Gulf
• VMA-211 (12 x AV-8B)
• VMA-311 (12 x AV-8B)

USS *Bataan*, Arabian Gulf
• VMA-223 (10 x AV-8B)
• VMA-542 (14 x AV-8B)

USS *Tarawa*, Arabian Gulf
• VMA-311 Detachment (6 x AV-8B)

USS *Nassau*, Arabian Gulf
• VMA-231 Detachment (6 x AV-8B)

pilot and forward air controllers could quickly confirm they were looking at the same target before authorising the release of weapons.

Operation Iraqi Freedom began on March 20, 2003, as US armoured columns crossed from Kuwait and headed north. I MEF columns operated on the eastern flank of the US drive towards Baghdad, first heading towards the southern city of Basra, then Nasiriyah, before pushing north to the capital.

Not surprisingly, USMC ground commanders wanted to have Harriers overhead constantly as they advanced into Iraq, to neutralise any pockets of resistance. So, 3 MAW commanders created special schedules to flow their Harriers over the battlefield. Jets were launched around the clock from Ahmed Al Jaber and the Harrier Carriers. Once they dropped their bombs, the jets turned around and headed back to Ahmed Al Jaber, where they were refuelled and rearmed, before being sent back north.

When I MEF columns reached Nasiriyah they ran into fanatical resistance from regular Iraqi army units, Ba'ath loyalists and militant Fedayeen groups. US vehicles were ambushed in the city's streets, resulting in numerous casualties a number of soldiers being taken prisoner. In these vicious street battles, the Harriers and their Litening II pods came into their own, finding and directing laser-guided bombs onto targets. When US special forces launched a rescue mission to free US POWs held in Nasiriyah, Harriers flew top cover and monitored the area around the objective with their targeting pods. For the first time the download facility was used so that the special forces commanders could see what was happening in the streets around the objective in real-time.

With the situation in Nasiriyah under control, I MEF now headed for Baghdad at a rapid pace. Iraqi resistance was starting to crumble, so there was little call for close air support from the Harriers. The attention of 3 MAW switched to attacking the reserve armoured divisions of the Iraqi Republican Guard. This was a classic battlefield air interdiction mission, striking »

AV-8Bs were held on strip alert at Al Assad Air Base in Iraq from 2004 to 2008 to support US Marines fighting insurgents in western Iraq.
US DoD/Combat Camera

BELOW: Ahmed Al Jaber Air Base was the hub for USMC Harrier operations during the invasion of Iraq in 2003.
Tim Ripley

at the enemy second and third echelon reserves.

The zone where the Republican Guard was located was divided into 'kill boxes' and each was patrolled by a forward air control jet that circled over Iraqi troop positions, handing off targets to inbound strike jets. This was a very different process from 1991, because the majority of the US and British jets now had targeting pods that made it far easier to find Iraqi tanks and designate laser-guided bombs. Over the course of a week, the Harriers and other

coalition jets worked over the Iraqi divisions, destroying hundreds of tanks, and prompting thousands of Iraqi soldiers to flee from the unrelenting air assault.

USMC commanders were keen to maintain the tempo of their advance and ensure that air support was always available, so 3 MAW began looking to forward-basing their Harriers in central Iraq. Harriers started to use Iraqi roads as improvised refuelling points. Then I MEF captured An Numaniyah airfield and turned it into a FARP

for Harriers and helicopters. Fuel and bombs were shuttled forward from Kuwait to the FARP in USMC Lockheed KC-130T Hercules airlifters.

As I MEF columns reached the outskirts of Baghdad, the Harriers switched back to close air support so they could organise air strikes within minutes as the marines fought through the streets of the Iraqi capital. It took US troops three days to push into the heart of Baghdad, using numerous Harrier strikes to break the back of Iraqi resistance. Again, the Litening II equipped

ABOVE: Concrete revetments were installed at Ahmed Al Jaber Air Base to protect Harriers from Iraqi Scud missile attacks.
Tim Ripley

RIGHT: Harrier pilots lived alongside their US Marine infantry comrades during their residence at Al Assad Air Base.
US DoD/Combat Camera

jets were able to find and hit small targets in the confused street fighting in Baghdad.

By April 10, Saddam Hussein had fled the capital and resistance had collapsed. A column of USMC troops was dispatched to capture the Iraqi leader's home city, Tikrit, with Harriers flying top cover. The city was captured on April 15 and, within a few weeks, I MEF and 3 MAW had started to head home. US President George W Bush famously welcomed home the aircraft carrier, USS *Abraham Lincoln* off the coast of »

California, giving a morale boosting speech to her crew under a banner infamously declaring 'Mission accomplished'.

Back in Iraq, insurgents did not get the 'mission accomplished' memo and started attacking US and coalition troops across the country. In the spring of 2004, US Marines were sent back to try to pacify a region to the west of Baghdad. When four American civilian security contractors were ambushed and killed by insurgents in the city of Fallujah in April 2004, the call went out for more air support. Ten AV-8Bs of VMA-542 took up residence at Al Assad Airbase in western Iraq, before VMA-214 arrived with another 10 jets.

Over the next six months, I MEF closed the noose around Fallujah in the build-up to a major ground assault to clear the city of insurgents in November 2004. The city was pummelled with more than 800 bombs and missiles, as well as 93,000 cannon rounds from US fast jets. During the final assault, AV-8Bs were constantly overhead providing close air support. The Harrier pilots were now experts at using their Litening II pods to locate and hit targets in narrow Iraqi back streets, leading the technique to be dubbed 'keyhole CAS' after the surgical procedure.

The recapture of Fallujah dealt a heavy blow to the insurgents, but they soon bounced back and upped the intensity of their revolt against the US occupation. For another four years, AV-8B squadrons took turns to deploy to Al Assad to support USMC

ABOVE: The USS *Nassau* was one of four 'Harrier Carriers' deployed to the Arabian Gulf for the invasion of Iraq in 2003. US DoD/ Combat Camera

BELOW LEFT: Twenty-four Harriers operated from the USS *Bataan* during Operation Iraqi Freedom. US DoD/ Combat Camera

LEFT: An AV-8B lifts off from Al Assad Air Base during the 2006 US troop surge that broke the back of the Iraqi insurgency.
US DoD/Combat Camera

troops operating west of Baghdad. For six months at a time, the Harrier squadrons stood alert ready to scramble to provide close air support to US Marines under attack. On a daily basis, they were also tasked to act as an 'eye in the sky', using their Litening II pods to aid Marine patrols.

USMC forward air controllers now had a more advanced version of the video downlink, dubbed a ROVER terminal. They would task Harrier pilots to fly their aircraft over areas of interest, looking for improvised explosive devises or insurgent ambushes. This saved numerous US lives as ground units were able to stay out of threat envelopes until the insurgents were neutralised.

The AV-8B squadrons were very much in the heart of the action, as Al Assad Airbase regularly came under mortar and rocket attack. By autumn 2008, the uprising had been calmed and US troops handed over responsibility to the Iraqis in much of the country. The security situation had so improved by October 2008 that the last AV-8B squadron, VMA-311, was able to return home, ending nearly five-and-a-half years of involvement of Harriers in Iraq.

BELOW: Operation Iraqi Freedom saw the Harrier transformed into a precision strike platform thanks to the widespread installation of Litening II targeting pods.
Tim Ripley

IRAQ 2003

RAF Harriers in Operation Telic

RIGHT: Inert practice bombs were pressed into service to reduce collateral damage during missions supporting US troops advancing through Baghdad.
Tim Ripley

In early 2003, more 40,000 British personnel were on their way to Iraq as part of the coalition to topple Saddam Hussein. The RAF deployed 8,000 RAF personnel to nine main operating bases in an arc from RAF Akrotiri on Cyprus through Jordan, Saudi Arabia, the Gulf States and down to Oman. Some 115 fixed wing combat, reconnaissance and transport aircraft were in place by March 2003.

RAF officers in the Middle East had been drawn into US plans for the air campaign against Iraq for several months and key roles were given to RAF Harrier squadrons in the war plans. A dozen Harriers of IV (Army Co-operation) and 1 (Fighter) Squadrons flew to Al Jaber Air base in Kuwait in early 2003, but the most diplomatically sensitive element in the RAF lay-down was the activation of Azraq Air Base in Jordan to host Harrier GR7 close air support jets, Canberra RP9 photo reconnaissance aircraft and Chinook HC2 transport helicopters.

BELOW: The Harrier GR7s of 3 (Fighter) Squadron provided aerial firepower to coalition special force patrols in western Iraq.
Stuart Atha, via RAF

Operation Telic formally began at 1800hrs local time on March 19, 2003, when the rules of engagement for RAF aircraft patrolling the no-fly zones were changed to allow them to conduct offensive missions throughout Iraq. The coalition unleashed its 'shock and awe' air and missile strikes across the country to cripple the Iraqi armed forces just as US and British troops were launching their ground invasion.

At the heart of the American plans to topple Saddam Hussein was an audacious push by US Army and US Marine Corps tank columns towards the Iraqi capital of Baghdad. For the RAF commanders, pilots, and ground crews of IV Squadron at Ahmed Al Jaber Air Base in Kuwait, the drive on Baghdad saw them ramp up operations dramatically, with each of

RIGHT: Ground crews applied 'shark teeth' markings to the Harrier GR7s at Ahmed Al Jaber Air Base. Tim Ripley

RIGHT: The digital joint reconnaissance pod (DJRP) was used by Harrier GR7s when they were tasked with monitoring Iraqi troop movements. Tim Ripley

BELOW RIGHT: RAF Harriers that participated in Operation Telic sported an impressive tally of bomb markings. Tim Ripley

the 12 Harriers flying two missions each day. The crews considered themselves the RAF close air support specialists and almost all of those deployed to Kuwait had seen action in Kosovo in 1999.

When a US Army AH-64A Apache attack helicopter brigade was devastated by Iraqi anti-aircraft fire, with every rotorcraft taking hits and one being shot down, leading to the capture of the crew, fixed wing air support was ramped up further.

The USAF and Marine Corps began sending up F-15E Strike Eagles and F/A-18C/D Hornets to act as airborne forward air controllers (AFACs), who would patrol above 'kill boxes', monitoring the situation on the ground and handing off targets to other jets. The tank kill rate went up dramatically and some 700 attack missions a day were being flown over Iraq, with the majority of these hitting targets between Baghdad and Nasiriyah. The RAF Harriers were flying nearly 100 sorties each day, with each jet dropping all its weapons. Some 85% of the munitions involved were precision laser- or satellite-guided weapons and hit rates of more than 95% were recorded in a systematic effort to destroy resistance.

RAF Lockheed Tristar tankers were now flying deep into Iraqi airspace to refuel British and US jets, so they could remain on station over the 'kill boxes' for longer. This meant there was a near constant flow of aircraft over the Iraqi forces, with the end result being the devastation of the Iraqi regular army, Republican Guard and Special Republican Guard, »

LEFT: 3 (Fighter) Squadron was based at Azraq Air Base in Jordan during Operation Row.
Stuart Atha, via RAF

BELOW: A Maverick-armed Harrier GR7 prepares to launch from Azraq airbase in Jordan to support Special Forces operating in western Iraq.
MoD Crown Copyright

their combat effectiveness reduced to almost zero.

The majority of Harrier pilots took off not knowing what they would be striking and only receiving their targets once they were nearing the battle zone. Over a five-day period, the RAF Harriers concentrated on hitting the Republican Guard's Medina and Baghdad divisions, while the USMC Harriers focused on the Iraqi 6th Armoured Division north of Basra.

The Harrier pilots said they used all the weapons in their inventory, with 50% being laser-guided Paveway bombs, 15-20% Maverick television-guided munitions and 5% satellite-guided Enhanced Paveway bombs. The remainder were 'dumb' or unguided 1000lb bombs and 66 of the controversial RB755 cluster bombs, which were withdrawn from RAF service in 2008 after the British government signed the international ban on cluster weapons.

In the first days of April, when US troops entered Baghdad, the need for close air support increased exponentially as heavy street fighting broke out across the city. IV (AC) Squadron sent two pairs of jets a day for urban close air support, armed predominately with Enhanced Paveway bombs, which had a fuse that could be adjusted by the pilot to detonate at variable altitudes from the ground. For the first time, the Harriers used

a version of the Enhanced Paveway that had no explosive warhead. It was designed to be used close to friendly troops or civilians and relied on kinetic force to destroy targets such buildings or vehicles.

By the time Iraqi resistance in Baghdad collapsed, the Harriers in Kuwait had flown 367 offensive sorties, dropping 117 munitions, and had mounted 22 sorties with the Joint Reconnaissance Pod (JRP). As well as tanks and armoured vehicles, the Harriers attacked other targets, including parked aircraft, surface-to-air missile sites, radars, and a mine-laying vessel in Basra harbour.

A constant nightmare for the US and British governments was the possibility of the Iraqis repeating their Scud missile attacks on Israel, which had caused so many problems during the 1991 conflict. A strong RAF contingent was dispatched to Azraq Air Base in eastern Jordan to support the US and UK Special Forces teams that were to conduct operations inside Iraq to neutralise the Scud threat. Also at Azraq were Harrier GR7s of 3 (Fighter) Squadron and high-flying Canberra reconnaissance aircraft of 39 Squadron.

The US and UK Special Forces ground patrols had their own dedicated air protection. RAF Harriers were in action on a daily basis, repulsing Iraqi counterattacks and striking artillery positions and anti-aircraft defences. When the war ended, 3 (F) Squadron had flown 290 sorties and dropped 73 munitions.

The Special Forces troops fanning across western Iraq did not find any Scuds, but the confusion they caused made the Iraqis think US and British troops were launching a major offensive from Jordan. This prompted the Iraqis to divert troops from the southern front to counter the 'phantom' army in the western desert.

LEFT: Squadron Leader Ned Cullen of 3(F) Squadron climbs out of one of the Harrier GR7's after returning from a mission over Iraq.
MoD/Crown Copyright

BELOW: The Harrier GR7s at Ahmed Al Jaber Air Base made extensive use of precision guided munitions.
Tim Ripley

AFGHANISTAN 2004-2009

RAF GR7/9s fighting the Taliban from the air

ABOVE: RAF Harriers were kept on strip alert at Kandahar Airfield to scramble to provide close air support for coalition troops under attack across southwestern Afghanistan.
Tim Ripley

RIGHT: Afghanistan's mountainous terrain was the backdrop to RAF Harrier operations between 2004 and 2009. 1 (Fighter) Squadron/MoD Crown Copyright

Britain's war in Afghanistan from 2004 to 2014 saw RAF and Royal Navy Harrier pilots win more praise for their role in delivering close air support (CAS) to protect allied ground troops from Taliban attacks.

Day after day, Harrier pilots scrambled to strike at Taliban fighters besieging isolated British outposts. Many soldiers credited the aerial firepower – laser-guided bombs, rocket salvos and 30mm cannon fire – delivered by Harriers as being the only thing that prevented their positions being overrun. This added another chapter to the Harrier legend, yet just over a year after the return of the last RAF Harrier squadron from Afghanistan, the British government decided to scrap all the jump jets as part of a sweeping round of spending cuts.

British ministers made the decision to dispatch Joint Force Harrier (JFH) to Afghanistan in the summer of

ABOVE: To give Harrier pilots maximum tactical flexibility, their aircraft always carried a mix of weapons, including Enhanced Paveway guided weapons and 1,000lb 'dumb' bombs. 1 (Fighter) Squadron/MoD Crown Copyright

RIGHT: Once air operations intensified in the summer of 2006, the Harrier detachment's aircraft started to sport impressive numbers of 'bomb mission' markings. Tim Ripley

2004 as part of a plan to ease the burden on the US military, which was increasingly preoccupied with countering insurgent attacks in Iraq.

In August 2004, the Ministry of Defence (MOD) announced that six GR7 jets from 3 (Fighter) Squadron would immediately start deploying to Kandahar Airfield (KAF) in southwestern Afghanistan to replace a squadron of USMC AV-8Bs. The US-run airbase would be the home of British Harrier squadrons for a decade.

US and allied troops across southern Afghanistan were coming under increasing attacks by Taliban insurgents and coalition commanders wanted CAS to be rapidly available to get them out of trouble. As the RAF CAS experts, JFH was the obvious choice. RAF Harrier squadrons were also trained and equipped to operate in small detachments in war zones, with limited logistic support in rudimentary forward air bases.

Kandahar's location meant the RAF Harriers did not require air-to-air refuelling to reach their operational area, unlike every other NATO fast jet unit in theatre. In 2005 and 2006, Kandahar's runway was being ››

repaired, so the Harriers were the only NATO fast jets that could use the airfield. So rather than fly cab-rank patrols waiting to be called into action, the RAF Harrier crews were held on strip alert on the ground, ready to be called on if troops came under attack. Pilots and ground crews stood alert near their fully armed and fuelled jets and, as soon as a call for CAS was received from the battlefield, they raced to their jets to get them airborne. If everything went to plan the Harriers could be over troops under threat in less than an hour.

At first, the RAF Harrier pilots rarely dropped live ordnance but calls for CAS started to ramp up rapidly as the Taliban escalated its offensive. Each Harrier squadron took turns to serve four months at KAF. In October 2005, the Harrier detachment found itself under Taliban rocket attack, with a strike hitting 3 (F) Squadron's flightline. One Harrier was completely destroyed and another seriously damaged. Replacement aircraft were quickly dispatched to KAF to reinforce 3 (F) Squadron and plans were made to step up CAS operations in 2006 to protect British Paratroopers of 16 Air Assault Brigade when they arrived in Helmand province to the northwest of Kandahar.

During the summer of 2006, British Paratroopers found themselves fighting for their lives inside several bases, dubbed Platoon Houses, across Helmand Province. These had meant to be humanitarian hubs where aid was distributed to locals as part of a British strategy to win the population's 'hearts and minds'. Within days of the British troops deploying across Helmand,

OPERATION HERRICK – RAF HARRIER DETACHMENT KANDAHAR AIRFIELD	
3 (Fighter) Squadron	September to December 2004
1 (Fighter) Squadron	December 2004 to April 2005
IV (Army Co-operation)	April to July 2005
3 (Fighter) Squadron	July to October 2005
IV (Army Co-operation) Squadron	October to December 2005
1 (Fighter) Squadron	December 2005 to May 2006
IV (Army Co-operation) Squadron	May to September 2006
800 Naval Air Squadron	September 2006 to January 2007
1 (Fighter) Squadron	January to June 2007
IV (Army Co-operation) Squadron	June to October 2007
Naval Strike Wing	October 2007 to February 2008
IV (Army Co-operation) Squadron	February to April 2008
1 (Fighter) Squadron	April to August 2008
Naval Strike Wing	August to December 2008
IV (Army Co-operation) Squadron	December 2008 to April 2009
1 (Fighter) Squadron	April to June 2009

LEFT: The 1,000lb general purpose bombs and CRV7 70 mm rockets pods. Tim Ripley

BELOW: A rapid take-off from Kandahar Airfield by an RAF Harrier after a scramble. 1 (Fighter) Squadron/ MoD Crown Copyright

they had come under intense attack from thousands of Taliban fighters. Harrier CAS was called down by specially trained forward air controllers, known as Joint Terminal Attack Controllers (JTACs), who had laser rangefinders and ROVER terminals to highlight targets for Harrier pilots.

Fearing they could be overrun, Parachute Regiment commanders called for CAS from the Harrier GR7 detachment at KAF. Dramatic video started to emerge of Paratroopers on the roofs of their Platoon Houses watching air strikes land a few dozen metres away. RAF officers said the British armed forces had not experienced anything quite like it since the Korean War in the 1950s or the Normandy campaign in World War Two.

Answering the call during that first summer of combat was IV (Army Co-operation) Squadron. In August 2006, some 160 air strikes were employed in Helmand, with 100 of them alone being used to keep Taliban fighters from overrunning British, Danish and US troops besieged in the town of Musa Qaleh. There were so many calls for CAS during August and September 2006 that an emergency airlift of bombs and rockets had to be organised to deliver more munitions to KAF from depots in Britain.

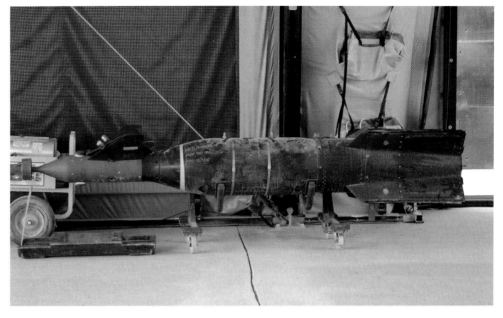

The IV (AC) Squadron pilots often did not know the precise locations of their targets before they took off and had to await calls for help from troops in contact or action with Taliban fighters to get detailed mission briefings. Because the fighting in Afghanistan took place largely in close proximity to ground troops, any targets for CAS had to be selected and authorised by JTACs working with British or allied ground troops before weapons could be released. These

were longstanding arrangements to prevent friendly fire that stretched back to World War Two.

Although the heavy fighting of 2006 was never repeated during the ten years of British combat operations in Afghanistan, the Taliban insurgency continued to spread across Helmand province and, by 2010, some 10,000 British troops were deployed across the region.

JFH's three RAF Harrier squadrons each took turns to spend four months at a time on duty in Afghanistan, **»**

ABOVE: The Enhanced Paveway II dual mode guided bomb gave RAF Harrier pilots a range of targeting options when trying to strike small groups of insurgents in Helmand Province. Tim Ripley

An IV (AC) Squadron Harrier and army mine proof vehicles at Kandahar Airfield, illustrating the proximity of the coalition air base to enemy forces. Tim Ripley

pod with the Lockheed Martin Sniper advanced targeting pod. This dramatically improved image quality and – crucially - allowed imagery to be downloaded from ROVER video terminals to allow JTACs to watch the high definition footage from the Harriers in real-time. This capability had the added benefit of allowing ground troops to use air assets as their own 'eye in the sky', to search behind hills or buildings for groups of Taliban fighters.

Over the course of its Operation Herrick commitment, JFH units flew some 8,640 sorties over 22,012 hours. Approximately 953 weapons were released by the Harriers, including 298 1,000lb Paveway IIs and 57 2,000lb Paveway IIIs. Non-guided weapons used included 1,000lb bombs and CVR-7 rockets.

By 2008, plans were made for JFH to stand down from Operation Herrick to allow its squadrons to take a well-earned rest. The Panavia GR4 Tornado squadrons had just finished their commitment to support Operation Telic in Iraq, so were available to replace JFH. They were equipped with the dual-mode MBDA Brimstone guided missile and the RAPTOR wide area surveillance pod.

In June 2009, 1 (F) Squadron handed over to 12 Squadron, bringing five years of Harrier operations in Afghanistan to an end.

ABOVE: Afghanistan's imposing geography never failed to impress RAF Harrier pilots.
1 (Fighter) Squadron/ MoD Crown Copyright

rotating the duty with the Fleet Air Arm (FAA) squadrons, until JFH was withdrawn to rest in the summer of 2009. The first FAA unit, 800 Naval Air Squadron, arrived at KAF in autumn of 2006, flying the same Harrier GR7s used by the RAF.

The Harriers were also progressively upgraded to improve their CAS capabilities, paving the way for the first GR9 variant to deploy in January 2007 with 1 (F) Squadron. Perhaps the most important improvement was the replacement of the old TIALD

RIGHT: Kandahar Air Field's bomb dump had to be massively expanded in 2006 as the conflict escalated.
Tim Ripley

AFGHANISTAN 2009-2013

USMC Harriers in Helmand Province

While the US Marine Corp's Harrier squadrons were writing a new chapter in jump jet history in Iraq between 2003 and 2008, the situation in Afghanistan was deteriorating under the weight of attacks by Taliban insurgents.

US commanders were recommending to US President Barack Obama that he send reinforcements to Afghanistan to turn around the situation. In the spring of 2009, Obama approved the dispatch of reinforcements, which became the known as 'The Surge'. Under the Pentagon's plans, US Marines were assigned to operate in southwestern Afghanistan alongside British, Canadian, and Dutch troops.

The 2nd Marine Expeditionary Brigade began deploying to Afghanistan in May 2009 and headed to the Garmsir district of Helmand Province to take over from hard-pressed British troops. Taliban insurgents were staging daily ambushes of Afghan government and coalition troops, as well regularly blowing up vehicles with improvised explosive devices (IEDs).

US Marine commanders were determined to move quickly to dominate their areas of responsibility and asked for AV-8B Harrier II support to be provided. In May 2009, VMA-214 arrived at Kandahar Airfield (KAF) with 10 Harriers. The huge airbase was the hub for US airpower in southwestern Afghanistan, with fast jets and

LEFT: Helmand Province's vast desert was the backdrop to four years of Harrier operations in southwest Afghanistan from 2009 to 2013. US DoD/Combat Camera

BELOW: USMC Harrier squadrons first deployed from the US-controlled base at Kandahar Airfield in 2009, before moving to Camp Bastion in 2012. US DoD/Combat Camera

helicopters to support coalition operations across the region.

Harriers stood alert at KAF ready to provide close air support (CAS) for US Marines who came under attack by Taliban fighters. Drawing on their experience in Iraq, the USMC Harrier pilots were tasked on a daily basis to provide top cover for ground patrols. Using Litening II targeting pods, they streamed video of the ground situation to forward air controllers (FACs) equipped with ROVER terminals. This 'eye in the sky' role, officially dubbed Non-Traditional Intelligence, Surveillance, and Reconnaissance

(NTISR), is credited with saving numerous lives by allowing coalition ground troops to pre-empt Taliban ambushes and IED attacks.

USMC AV-8Bs were now cleared to carry 1,000lb and 2,000lb versions of satellite-guided Joint Direct Attack Munition (JDAM) bombs. This allowed Harriers to attack targets with pinpoint accuracy, even in rain, dust storms or through cloud.

In February 2010, a major USMC operation was launched to seize the Marjah district and lavish air support was laid on to cover the troops as they moved into the Taliban »

ABOVE: The British-run Camp Bastion was built in the centre of the Helmand desert in 2006. US DoD/Combat Camera

BELOW: A crew chief clears an AV-8B to leave its revetment before taking off from Camp Bastion in 2012. US DoD/Combat Camera

ABOVE: Six AV-8Bs of VMA-211 were destroyed during the infamous Taliban attack on Camp Bastion in September 2012. US DoD/Combat Camera

stronghold. A 'CAS stack' was enacted over the town as the assault troops moved forward – this involved a constant orbit of Harriers from VMA-231 being on station, ready to be called forward by FACs to attack ground targets, with KC-10 Extender tankers providing air-to-air refuelling for the jets. A forward armed and refuelling point (FARP) was set up at the British-run Camp Bastion airfield to allow jets to be rapidly re-armed.

During Operation Moshtarak, the Harriers carried out more 25mm cannon strafing runs than bombing attacks in a bid to reduce collateral damage and civilian casualties. The kinetic phase of the operation only lasted a few days before the Taliban melted away to regroup.

The AV-8B squadrons were given a break from Afghan duty at KAF when VMA-231 was replaced for six months by an F/A-18C Hornet squadron. Harriers of VMA-513 arrived in KAF in May 2011.

In the spring of 2010, President Obama ordered a ramping up of The Surge and the USMC took over responsibility for the north of Helmand Province. A major operation was launched to clear insurgents from Sangin and Kajaki districts, with VMA-513 to the fore to provide air support. It took several months for the operation to unfold across the huge expanse of northern Helmand. VMA-513 flew 4,033 combat hours during 2,261 sorties, responding to 2,145 CAS requests and expending 81 precision-guided munitions. It also fired 4,737 rounds

RIGHT: Lieutenant Colonel Chris Raible, commanding officer of VMA 211, was killed leading his Marines into action at Camp Bastion. US DoD/ Combat Camera

ABOVE: Maintainers from VMA-513 preparing to launch AV-8Bs from Kandahar Airfield in 2011. US DoD/Combat Camera

of 25 mm ammunition in 50 strafing runs. The squadron also had made 59 show of force flybys, to try to scare off Taliban attackers.

The intensity of Harrier operations continued into 2012 as heavy fighting continued across Helmand. To reduce the reaction time to CAS requests, US Marine commanders ordered that the Harrier squadron move forward from KAF to Camp Bastion, which was now a major USMC base. In the space of a few weeks, USMC engineers built the facilities needed to allow

VMA-211, the famous 'Wake Island Avengers', to take up residence.

During the evening of September 14, 2012, a squad of Taliban sappers managed to penetrate the Camp Bastion perimeter fence to stage a daring attack on VMA-211's flightline. The attackers detonated explosive charges next to the squadron's Harriers and fired rocket-propelled grenades at the aircraft before its personnel knew what was happening. The squadron commanding officer, Lieutenant

Colonel Chris Raible, immediately rallied his Marine pilots and technicians to fight off the attack. Grabbing M16s, Raible and his troops traded fire for several hours to defend their position, living up to the USMC ethos, that 'Every Marine is a rifleman first'. By the time all the Taliban attackers had been killed or captured, VMA-211 had taken several casualties, including Raible and Sergeant Bradley Atwell, who were killed in action. The squadron's flightline was extensively damaged, with six AV-8Bs destroyed and two more badly damaged. This was the worst aircraft loss suffered by a USMC aviation squadron in a single day since World War Two. To get back in the fight rapidly, eight replacement Harriers were heading to Camp Bastion within days.

During 2013, troops involved in The Surge started to leave Afghanistan on President Obama's orders. To give the Afghan government's army the best chance once US and coalition troops left, a series of major sweeps were launched to clear out remaining Taliban pockets. USMC Harriers of VMA-231 supported these assaults, including dropping 51 JDAMs during an operation to clear a Taliban stronghold in Helmand. The honour of flying the very last AV-8B mission in Afghanistan fell to a pair of jets from VMA-311 on September 11, 2013. This was just under 12 years since the first AV-8B strikes in Afghanistan and ended an important chapter in jump jet history.

RIGHT: Close air support was the main mission of USMC Harriers during their Afghan campaign between 2009 and 2013. US DoD/Combat Camera

LIBYA 2011

USMC and Italian Harrier strikes on North Africa

For nearly five months in 2016, USMC Harriers pounded the city of Sirte from the USS *Wasp*. US DoD/Combat Camera

BELOW: Operation Odyssey Lightning in 2016 saw USMC AV-8Bs strike at Islamic State fighters in the Libyan city of Sirte. US DoD/ Combat Camera

Libya has special place in the history of the US Marine Corps (USMC), dating back to the Battle of Derna in 1805, when an expedition was launched to punish pirates for attacks on American ships. It even features in the Marines' Hymn, with the line to "From the halls of Montezuma to the shores of Tripoli". So, when USS *Kearsage* was dispatched to the Libyan coast in March 2011 to take part in a United Nations-sponsored campaign to protect the country's civilian population from attack by the army of Muammar Gaddafi, it generated great excitement among the US Marines onboard.

On March 20, AV-8B Harrier IIs of VMA-542 joined the opening strikes of Operation Odyssey Dawn, which was aimed at establishing a no-fly zone over the country. Two days later, a USAF F-15E crash-landed in Libya after a mechanical fault. To recover the two pilots, USMC MV-22B Osprey tiltrotors were launched from USS *Kearsage*, with Harriers flying top cover. As the marines landed and secured the pilots, the AV-8Bs flew patrols around the location, strafing potentially hostile vehicles with cannon fire and dropping two 500lb laser-guided bombs.

A growing armada of international warships arrived off the Libyan coast to support the air offensive. This included the Italian aircraft carrier, ITS *Giuseppe Garibaldi*, with eight AV-8B Plus embarked, arriving on station on March 24. The jets took part in several patrols off the Libyan coast until Gaddafi's regime fell in November, flying 1,221 hours and dropping 160 laser guided bombs. The Italian AV-8Bs also took part in combat air patrols to enforce the UN-mandated no-fly zone.

Despite western military intervention and the fall of Gaddafi, Libya remained a chaotic failed state, with rival militia and Islamic State (IS) insurgents controlling large parts of the country. By August 2016, US intelligence was detecting a build-up of IS fighters in the coastal city of Sirte in eastern Libya. Local fighters had pushed the IS forces into the city and US airpower from the USS *Wasp* was unleashed to quash the uprising.

RIGHT: ITS *Giuseppe Garibaldi* launched its Harriers into action against targets in Libya during the 2011 conflict. US Navy

Over five months, the US military conducted Operation Odyssey Lightning, with Harriers of VMA-542 striking IS targets. Its AV-8Bs dropped 290 laser-guided bombs during nearly 500 sorties – the most intense period of air strikes ever launched solely from a US Navy amphibious ship.

Libyan operations by US and Italian Harriers showed the potential of 'Harrier Carriers' to support small scale interventions where a full 'cats and traps' carrier was not needed. Most of the country's population lived in coastal cities, so this was an ideal scenario for Harrier Carriers, because their jets could hit the majority of targets without requiring air-to-air refuelling.

Italian and US Harrier Carriers also embarked attack and transport helicopters, so they could launch a range of missions off the Libyan coast, including raids against high-value targets and perform combat search and rescue of downed pilots.

BELOW: Nighttime attacks from Harriers embarked on USS *Wasp* ensured Islamic State fighters had no respite during the 2016 siege of Sirte. US DoD/ Combat Camera

AFGHANISTAN AND SYRIA 2018-2021

A new generation of F-35B jump jets go to war

The US Marine Corps (USMC) and allied air arms began receiving their first Lockheed Martin F-35B Lightning IIs in 2012, but it took several years for the jets to be declared fully operational.

In September 2018, the first combat air strike by F-35Bs was carried out in Afghanistan by the USMC. US military advisors and forward air controllers worked with Afghan government troops trying to secure the Salma Dam in Herat Province. Bad weather grounded USAF jets at Bagram Airbase, so the call went out to VMFA-211 'Wake Island Avengers' on the amphibious ship USS *Essex* to strike Taliban fighters threatening America's allies. The F-355Bs hit their targets at night and reportedly took the Taliban by surprise, causing considerable damage and allowing the Afghan troops to advance.

British F-35Bs made their first deployment on May 22, 2019, when six Lightnings from 617 Squadron 'Dambusters' arrived at the British airbase at RAF Akrotiri, Cyprus, for

six weeks as part of Exercise Lightning Dawn. On June 16, 2019, 617 Squadron carried out the RAF's first ever F-35 operational mission when two Lightnings conducted a patrol over Syria as part of Operation Shader. The aircraft were refuelled in the air on a number of occasions by A330 Voyager tanker aircraft. No bombs were dropped during the sorties.

A few days later, the Dambuster's F-35Bs participated in Exercise

Tri-Lightning alongside USAF F-35As of the 4th Fighter Squadron and Israeli Air Force F-35Is of 140 Squadron over the eastern Mediterranean.

In June 2021, 617 Squadron was in action over Syria, this time flying from the Royal Navy's newest aircraft carrier, HMS *Queen Elizabeth*. The ship was passing through Mediterranean en route to the Pacific as part of the Carrier Strike Group 2021 (CSG21) deployment.

USMC F-35Bs of VMA-211 were also embarked on HMS *Queen Elizabeth*. The British and US jets did not drop any bombs during the missions over Syria.

Captain James Blackmore, commander of HMS *Queen Elizabeth's* Carrier Air Wing, said the patrols over Syria marked the Royal Navy's return to maritime strike operations: "With its fifth-generation capabilities, including outstanding situational awareness, the F-35B is the ideal aircraft to deliver precision strikes, which is exactly the kind of mission that 617 Squadron has been training for day after day, night after night, for these past few months. This is also notable as the first combat mission flown by US aircraft from a foreign carrier since HMS *Victorious* in the South Pacific in 1943. The level of integration between Royal Navy, RRAF and USMC is truly seamless, and testament to how close we've become since we first embarked together last October."

The CSG21 cruise also saw Britain and America stand deck alert to fly fleet defence missions in the Mediterranean in November 2021. They were scrambled on several occasions when Russian Sukhoi fighters based in Syria made forays towards the British carrier.

In the summer of 2025, HMS *Prince of Wales* will sail to the Far East, and this will no doubt see her F-35Bs taking to the skies again to protect the carrier strike group as it cruises through the Mediterranean, Middle East, and South China Sea.

THE RED SEA
2023-2024

The Harrier's last hurrah?

When Hamas fighters breached Israel's border wall around the Gaza Strip on October 7, 2023, it set off a chain of events that rapidly escalated into a conflict that spread across the Middle East. Houthi rebels in Yemen declared their support for the Palestinians and said they would attack any Israeli ships in the Red Sea. On October 19, 2023, USS *Carney* on patrol off Yemen shot down four cruise missiles and 15 drones over a period of nine hours. Within weeks, attacks on merchant shipping in the Red Sea were happening on a daily basis, one being captured by Houthi commandos who landed by helicopter.

US Central Command decided to reinforce its naval patrols in the Red Sea and dispatched the USS *Bataan* Amphibious Ready Group (ARG), as well as other warships, to uphold freedom of navigation. USS *Bataan* stayed on station in the centre of the Red Sea for two months, with its US Marine Corps (USMC) AH-1Y Cobra attack helicopters and AV-8B Harrier II jump jets flying patrols to deter Houthi attacks.

A series of engagement zones were set up along the Red Sea coast so Houthi missiles and drones could be rapidly intercepted. One AV-8B pilot was credited with intercepting seven Houthi drones, although it is not clear if he shot them down or caused them to miss their targets. Captain Earl Ehrhart of Marine Attack

The Houthi attacks steadily escalated, prompting the US to launch Operation Prosperity Guardian to better co-ordinate international naval forces in the region. Iranian-backed militia groups had also stepped up drone and rocket attacks on US bases across Iraq and Syria. To deter further escalation, the US Navy dispatched the USS *Dwight D Eisenhower* to the Arabian Gulf to launch her jets on combat air patrols over the two countries.

After the USS *Bataan* ARG sailed north through the Suez Canal on December 28, she was replaced in the Red Sea by the USS *Dwight D Eisenhower*. This ended the Harrier's role in the crisis, which might very well be the famous jump jets last combat outing in USMC service.

Squadron 231 (VMA-231) 'Ace of Spades' told the BBC in an interview: "We took a Harrier jet and modified it for air defence, we loaded it up with missiles and that way were able to respond to their drone attacks."

JUMP JET SQUADRONS

All the world's VTOL combat aircraft squadrons and units

INDIAN NAVAL AIR ARM

ABOVE: Indian Navy Sea Harriers regularly carried out exercises with international partners in the Indian Ocean.
US Navy

RIGHT: India's Sea Harrier heritage is proudly on display at the country's Naval Aviation Museum in Goa.
Aryan Bhutani

India has a long history of operating British-made aircraft, so it was not a surprise when it placed its first order for six Sea Harrier FRS.51 fighters and two T.60 Trainers in November 1979 to replace its British-built Hawker Sea Hawk jets. Its Sea Harriers were essentially similar to Royal Navy FRS.1s, but with Matra R550 Magic air-to-air missiles. These aircraft were later upgraded with the Elta EL/M-2032 radar and Rafael Derby beyond visual range missiles.

The first three Sea Harriers arrived in India on December 16, 1983. Ten more were ordered two years later, and eventually a total of 30 jets were purchased, including five two-seat trainers. The aircraft initially operated from INS *Vikrant*, before

transferring to INS *Viraat* (formerly HMS *Hermes*) in 1987.

Until the 1990s, significant portions of pilot training were carried out in Britain due to limited aircraft availability, which prompted the Indian Navy to form a dedicated training unit.

The sole Indian Navy Sea Harrier unit, Indian Naval Air Squadron 300, operated the jet until it was retired from service in 2016, to make way for the Mikoyan MiG-29.

INS *Viraat* and her Sea Harriers played a leading role in several high-profile Indian military interventions, starting with Operation Jupiter in July 1989 to deliver a peacekeeping force to the island state Sri Lanka, off India's southern tip.

After gunmen attacked the Indian parliament in December 2021, the New Delhi government blamed Pakistani-based Kashmiri militants and a full-scale mobilisation of the Indian armed forces was ordered. Operation Parakram saw more than 800,000 Indian military personnel mass on the Pakistan border and INS *Viraat* was moved into position to lead a naval blockade against Pakistani ports. Diplomacy resolved the crisis, but it showed how the Indians intended to use their aircraft carrier to dominate the sea zone off its neighbour.

This was the closest India's Sea Harriers got to seeing action before they were withdrawn from service.

Unit: Indian Naval Air Squadron 300
Nickname/Motto: The White Tigers
Home Base: INS Hansa

Aircraft
Sea Harrier FRS51/60: 1984-2016

Unit: Indian Naval Air Squadron 551B/552
Nickname/Motto: The Phantoms (INAS 551), The X-plorers (INAS 552)
Home Base: INS Hansa

Aircraft
Sea Harrier FRS51/60: 1990-2014

ITALIAN NAVAL AVIATION

The ITS *Cavour* embarked both the AV-8B Plus and F-35B for her long-range cruise to the Far East in the summer of 2024. Italian Navy

Italy did not have a fully functional aircraft carrier until ITS *Guiseppe Garibaldi* was commissioned in 1985. The carrier was ordered in 1981 to fulfil Italy's strategic naval operations along with AV-8B Harrier II Plus jets in 1989, after the country's laws were changed to allow the Marina Militare to operate fixed wing aircraft.

The Marina Militare acquired its Harriers to use as fleet defence aircraft to protect its warships at sea from air attack, with actual strike operations against land targets as a secondary priority. In addition, its aircraft carriers are used in humanitarian operations and diplomatic visits, and as a show of the country's strength and prestige.

With the ending of the Cold War, the Marina Militare had to reassess its operational concepts, finding its aircraft carriers were useful in what soon became known as the 'new world disorder'. The ITS *Giuseppe Garibaldi* has been used in a variety of roles, including as a strike carrier to attack land targets in support of Italian and allied peacekeeping troops.

Italy was one of the first international partners to join the

BELOW: Italy selected the AV-8B Plus as its first-ever carrier-borne combat aircraft. Aldo Bidini

LEFT: Italian
Harrier pilots
train on the
TAV-8B before
transitioning to
the operational
squadron. Future
F-35B pilots
will not have
this luxury as
there is no two-
seat version, so
simulators will fill
this training gap.
US DoD/US Navy

project to build the F-35 Lightning II joint strike fighter. The Marina Militare ordered 15 F-35B jump jet variants to operate from its carriers, with the first being delivered in 2018. ITS *Cavour,* home ported at Taranto with the 2nd Naval Division in the strike carrier role, sailed across the Atlantic in the spring of 2021 to carry out integration trials with aircraft

of the US F-35 Integrated Test Task Force. These proved that the carrier could safely embark and operate the F-35B. Initial operating capability was expected to be declared in late 2024, to make the full transition of the Marina Militare from the AV-8B to the F-35B. The activation of ITS *Cavour* as a Lightning carrier will allow the retirement of the AV-8B.

Service: Italian Marina Militare, Aviazione Navale
Unit: Gruppo Aerei Imbarcati – GRUPAER
Home Base: Taranto-Grottaglie Airport

Aircraft
AV-8B Plus: 1991 to date
F-35B: 2017 to date

BELOW: The F-35B
is now entering
service with the
Italian Navy to
replace the AV-8B.
Presidenza della
Repubblica

JAPANESE AIR SELF DEFENSE FORCE

Japan has a long tradition of naval aviation, stretching back to the 1920s, when the Imperial Japanese Navy saw the potential of carrier-borne aviation as a war winning weapon to overturn US naval dominance in the Pacific. Japan's defeat in 1945 and subsequent US occupation led to the country being disarmed. When the US allowed Japan to begin rebuilding its armed forces in the 1950s, the country disavowed the ownership of offensive weapons, which was taken to include aircraft carriers and amphibious forces.

However, over the past 25 years, the modern Japanese Maritime Self Defence Force (JMSDF) has been steadily building up its naval capability as tension has grown with China. The JMSDF has started building up its amphibious forces to allow ground troops to be moved to Japanese islands in the western Pacific or to land marines to retake them. Work has started to convert the amphibious landing ship JS *Izumo* and its sister ship, JS *Kaga*, into what the JMSDF terms 'light aircraft carriers' or 'Lightning carriers', to allow them to lead a combined air-land task force.

In December 2018, the Japanese government announced that it would buy 42 F-35B Lightning IIs so they could be embarked on the Izumo-class ships. Plans were made to convert JS *Izumo* and JS *Kaga* to each carry up to 14 F-35Bs. The first of these aircraft are due to be delivered during 2025 and they will be under the command of the Japanese Air Self Defence Force's 5th Air Wing. Although the F-35B will operate from JMSDF ships, the airframes and personnel are under JASDF command. A dedicated training site is to be set up on the island of Mageshima, including a mock-up of an Izumo-class ship's flight deck to allow F-35B pilots to practice take-offs and landings.

Later in 2024, one of the Izumo-class ships headed to the Eastern seaboard of the US to carry out integration trials with Lightning aircraft of the US F-35 Integrated Test Force. This is the same process followed by British and Italian aircraft carriers to allow them to safely operate the F-35B. Once full safety clearances have been established, the JASDF aircraft will be able to take its aircraft to sea and re-establish Japan's aircraft carrier capability.

Unit: 5th Air Wing.
Home Base: Nyutabaru Air Base

Aircraft
F-35B from 2025

SOVIET NAVAL AVIATION

ABOVE: Soviet Naval Aviation operated the Yak-38 from 1976 to 1992. US Navy

BELOW: Kiev-class aircraft carriers embarked the Yak-38 as part of their air groups. US Navy

The Soviet Navy's (AV-MF) aviation branch operated the Yakovlev Yak-38 from 1976 until the collapse of the USSR in 1992. They were the fixed wing element embarked on Kiev-class aircraft carriers. Once fully in service, the aircraft operated in the Northern and Pacific fleets, each assigned its own Independent Shipboard Attack Air Regiment (OKShAP). Training was the responsibility of the 279 OKShAP based at Saki in Crimea. The first of class, *Kiev*, joined the Northern Fleet in 1976 and the other two

carriers, *Minsk* and *Novorossiysk*, entered service soon after.

In July 1979, *Minsk* arrived in the Sea of Japan, where the vessel was home-ported at Strelok Bay, the Yak-38 component of its air wing thereafter being provided by the 311 OKShAP subordinate to the Pacific Fleet.

In September 1982, *Novorossiysk* was commissioned. By now the V/STOL technique had been well practised and the resulting increase in the Yak-38's overall performance and capability was exploited during the passage of *Novorossiysk* from Severomorsk to join the Pacific Fleet.

A pair of armed Yak-38s operating from *Minsk* intercepted aircraft from the USS *Enterprise* over the Arabian Sea on December 16, 1982. This event marked the first time Soviet VTOL aircraft had intercepted US aircraft while armed with missiles.

In a maritime context, the Yak-38 was not limited to *Kiev*. In September 1983, AV-MF pilots operated from the civilian Ro-Ro vessel *Agostinho Neto*, while NII-VVS (Air Force Scientific Test Institute) pilots conducted further tests from another Ro-Ro vessel, *Nikolai Cherkasov*.

In 1992, the new Russian Federation Navy withdrew its Kiev-class carriers from service and the Yak-38s were scrapped.

Unit: 279 OKShAP (Otdelny Korabelny Shturmovoy Aviatsionny Polk; Independent Shipboard Attack Air Regiment)
Home Base: Saki, Severomorsk-3.

Aircraft
Yak-38/38M: 1973-1991

Unit: 299 IIAP (Issledovatlesko-Instruktorskiy Aviatsionnyi Polk; Research and Instructor Air Regiment)
Home Base: Saki

Aircraft
Yak-38/38M: 1976-1991

Unit: 311 OKShAP (Otdelny Korabelny Shturmovoy Aviatsionny Polk; Independent Shipboard Attack Air Regiment)
Home Base: Pristan, Primorskiy

Aircraft
Yak-38/38M: 1976-1992

SPANISH NAVAL AVIATION

In 1972, Hawker Siddeley flew a Harrier to Spain to make a test landing on the SPS *Dédalo*'s wooden flight deck. After the successful test, the US helped persuade the British to sell the Armada Española a batch of Harriers, which they dubbed the AV-8S Matador. The aircraft were in operational service on SPS *Dédalo* in 1976, three years before the Royal Navy's Sea Harrier FRS1 entered service on British aircraft carriers, making Spain the first European navy to operate a 'Harrier Carrier'.

Spain joined NATO in 1982 and, since then, its aircraft carriers have participated in numerous alliance exercises around the Mediterranean and Atlantic regions. The SPS *Dédalo* was replaced by the home-built SPS *Príncipe de Asturias* in 1988. She embarked the upgraded EAV-8B Matador, essentially an AV-8B Harrier II Plus, and was fitted with a ski-jump to enhance their operational performance.

The ship remained in service until 2012, when a new class of light carrier/amphibious assault ship entered service. The SPS *Juan Carlos I* was laid down in 2005 and was initially known as a Strategic Projection Vessel because of her multi-role capabilities. Her crew of 900 can be complemented by another 1,200 marines or passengers. The ship is based at Rota Naval Base as part of Naval Action Group 2, which also includes Spain's amphibious landing ships. Her air wing is based nearby at Rota's military air base.

The Spanish Navy's remaining dozen or so EAV-8Bs are long due to be replaced, but the Madrid government has put off deciding on whether to buy the only viable option, the F-35B Lightning II. Italy and the USMC will both retire their last AV-8Bs over the next two years, leaving Spain the only operator of the aircraft until its planned retirement in 2030.

There has been speculation that the Spanish government could soon launch a major rearmament plan that would include the purchase of between 12 and 25 F-35Bs for the SPS *Juan Carlos I*, but no official confirmation has been made public.

Units: 8 Escuadrilla (AV-8S), 9 Escuadrilla (AV-8B Plus)
Home Base: Rota

Aircraft
AV-8S Matador: 1976-1996
AV-8B Plus: 1987 to date

ROYAL THAI NAVY AIR DIVISION

RIGHT: Thailand bought Spain's surplus AV-8S in 1997, but they only remained in service for less than a decade because of spares and training shortfalls. Z3144228

In 1992, the Royal Thai Navy (RTN) ordered the new light aircraft carrier HTMS *Chakri Naruebet* from Spain to bolster its then largely coastal fleet, giving Thailand a power projection capability for the first time. As part of the procurement, ten of the Spanish AV-8S Matadors, an export version of the first-generation Harriers, were sold to the RTN by Madrid.

HTMS *Chakri Naruebet* was fitted with an aircraft ski-jump and the initial intention was to operate a mixed group of AV-8S Matadors and Sikorsky SH-60 Seahawk helicopters. Unfortunately, the delivery of the carrier and its accompanying air wing in 1998 coincided with an Asian financial crisis, which resulted in the RTN being unable to procure any spare parts for the Matadors, forcing them to cannibalise the aircraft to keep them flying. By 1999, it was reported that only one Matador was operational

due to parts, training, and fiscal limitations, although three of the type were spotted on the ship on January 29, 2003 during a show of force after the riots in Phnom Penh, Cambodia.

In 2006, after just eight years of service, the RTN retired all of its remaining AV-8Ss from service in favour of repurposing HTMS *Chakri*

BELOW: HMTS *Chakri Naruebet* embarked Thailand's AV-8Ss until they were retired in 2006. US Navy

Naruebet into a helicopter carrier, concluding the service of the first-generation Harriers.

Unit: HTMS *Chakri Naruebet* Flying Unit
Home Base: U-Tapao RTNAB

Aircraft
AV-8S Matador: 1997-2006

ROYAL AIR FORCE
1 (FIGHTER) SQUADRON

RIGHT: 1 (F) Squadron played a key role in the Afghan campaign, flying the Harrier GR7 and later the GR9. 1(F) Squadron/ MoD Crown Copyright

RIGHT: When the British overseas territory of Belize was threatened by neighbouring Guatemala in 1975, 1 (F) Squadron dispatched six Harrier GR3s that remained until 1993. Pete Butt

1 (Fighter) Squadron can trace its history back to 1912, when the unit was formed as part of the Royal Flying Corps, the British Army's first aviation arm. It has a long association with the Harrier jump jet, being the RAF's first operation squadron to fly the revolutionary aircraft in 1969, making it the world's first vertical take-off and landing jet squadron.

During its first two decades operating the Harrier, the squadron had a global rapid reaction role

RIGHT: HMS Hermes was the home for 1 (F) Squadron in May and June 1982 for Operation Corporate to liberate the Falkland Islands. MoD/Crown Copyright

supporting NATO and Britain's allies. Its first operational deployment occurred in 1975, when six of the squadron's Harrier GR3 jets were flown to Belize in Central America, when neighbouring Guatemala threatened the self-governing British territory.

In 1982, the squadron took part in the British campaign to recover the Falkland Islands, achieving many firsts. It embarked on the carrier HMS *Hermes* after a transit to the South Atlantic on the converted container ship SS *Atlantic Conveyer*. Harrier GR4s led the bombing campaign against Argentinian troops, including making decisive bombing attacks on the garrison of Goose Green. In a major milestone, 1 (F) Squadron was the first RAF unit to use laser-guided bombs in action against an Argentine troop position.

It was also the first Harrier unit to transition to the Harrier GR5 in 1988, and over the next 22 years operated the GR5/7/9 variants of the jump jet in several operational theatres, including Bosnia, Iraq, and Afghanistan. The squadron joined Joint Force Harrier in 2000, then moved to RAF Cottesmore as part of a consolidation of RAF and RN Harrier units at the station.

It ceased flying the Harrier in December 2010 after the retirement of the last aircraft but was resurrected in 2012 as a Eurofighter Typhoon unit.

Nickname/Motto: In omnibus princeps (First in all things)
Home Base: RAF Wittering (1969-2000), RAF Cottesmore (2000-2010)

Aircraft
Harrier GR1/3: 1969-1988
Harrier GR5/7/7A: 1988-2006
Harrier GR9/9A: 2006-2010

3 (FIGHTER) SQUADRON

**ABOVE: 3 (F)
Squadron began
receiving its first
Harrier GR5 jets
in December 1988.**
Szilas

Originally formed as part of the Royal Flying Corps in 1912, 3 (Fighter) Squadron saw extensive service in the ground attack role in World War Two, flying the Hawker Typhoon.

After World War Two, it became one of the core units of RAF Germany (RAFG), supporting NATO forces during the Cold War. In 1972, it converted to the Harrier GR3 as part of the RAFG's Harrier Force, with the role of operating from field sites in support of the British Army of the Rhine (BAOR). This role entailed Harrier squadrons deploying to camouflaged hides in woods or industrial sites to avoid potential

Soviet air attacks. Harrier squadrons operated with minimal ground support, to allow them to be based close to the frontline and respond rapidly for calls for close air support.

After transitioning to the GR5/7 variant in 1989, 3 (F) Squadron participated in many live operations during the 1990s, including over the Balkans and Iraq, policing no-fly zones, mainly in the tactical reconnaissance role. The squadron saw action in the 2003 Iraq war, flying in support of US, UK, and Australian special forces in western Iraq. It was also the first British Harrier unit to deploy to Afghanistan in 2004, taking its turn to serve at Kandahar Airfield until 2006 for Operation Herrick.

As part of the drawdown of Joint Force Harrier and following the retirement of the Sea Harrier in 2006, the squadron handed over its jets to 800 Naval Air Squadron, then transitioned to the Eurofighter Typhoon.

Unit: 3 (Fighter) Squadron
Nickname/Motto: Tertius primus erit (The third shall be the first)
Home Base: RAF Wildenrath (1972-1977), RAF Gutersloh (1977-1992), RAF Laarbuch (1992-2000), RAF Cottesmore (2000-2006)

Aircraft
Harrier GR1/3: 1972-1991
Harrier GR5/7/7A: 1991-2006

**RIGHT: The Harrier
GR3 variant was
operated by 3 (F)
Squadron between
1972 and 1991.**
Anidaat

IV (ARMY CO-OPERATION) SQUADRON

Like the other original RAF Harrier units, IV (Army Co-operation) Squadron has a distinguished pedigree, dating back to 1912 and the formation of the Royal Flying Corps.

After World War Two it remained in the ground attack role, with de Havilland Vampires, North American Sabres and Hawker Hunters. Thus, when the squadron converted to the Harrier GR1 in 1970 as part of RAF Germany (RAFG), it was a natural progression.

Along with 3 (Fighter) Squadron and 20 Squadron, IV (AC) Squadron operated the Harrier GR1/3 from dispersed field sites in the 1970s as part of the Harrier Force. After the end of the Cold War, the Harrier Force assumed a global role, with IV (AC) Squadron being the first Harrier unit to deploy to Incirlik airbase in Turkey for Operation Warden in 1993. In 1995, it was the first Harrier squadron to support the United Nations in Bosnia, and in August and September of that year used laser-guided bombs for the first time from the GR7 during Operation Deliberate Force. It was the lead Harrier unit in Kuwait for Operation Telic in 2003 and, three years later, was in the thick of the action in southern Afghanistan after

British troops came under heavy Taliban attack.

The squadron continued to operate the Harrier in the attack role until March 2010, when it was disbanded. Its number plate was immediately transferred to the Harrier operational conversion unit, 20 (Reserve) Squadron, to become IV (Reserve) Squadron. By the end of the year, it was out of business as a Harrier unit after the aircraft were retired in a round of budget cuts, but, in 2011, it was resurrected as an advanced jet training unit flying the Hawk T2 at RAF Valley.

Unit: IV (Army Co-operation) Squadron, IV (Reserve) Squadron (2010)
Nickname/Motto: In futurum videre (To see into the future)
Home Base: RAF Wittering (1970), RAF Wildenrath (1970-1977), RAF Gutersloh (1977-1992), RAF Laarbuch (1992-2000), RAF Cottesmore (2000-2010), RAF Wittering (2010)

Aircraft
Harrier GR1/3: 1970-1989
Harrier GR5/7/7A: 1989-2006
Harrier GR9/9A: 2006-2010

RIGHT:
20 Squadron was the Harrier operational conversion unit from 1992 to 2010, training a generation of jump jet pilots.
MoD/Crown Copyright

20 SQUADRON

BELOW: Two-seat versions of the Harrier were concentrated at RAF Wittering, to allow student pilots to learn how to fly the unique jump jet.
Anthony Noble

Converting to the Harrier in 1970, 20 Squadron operated the GR1 and GR3 variants until 1977, when a rationalisation of RAF Germany led it to being disbanded. It was resurrected in 1992 as the Harrier operational conversion unit (OCU) after 233 OCU was re-badged as 20 (Reserve) Squadron at RAF Wittering. The station had long been seen as the home of the Harrier because 233 OCU and 1 (Fighter) Squadron had been based there since 1969.

Using two-seat versions of the jump jet, 233 OCU played a key role in preparing RAF pilots for frontline duty by teaching them how to make the most of the Harrier's unique characteristics. As well as converting RAF airmen to fly the jump jet, it also instructed pilots to fly Royal Navy Sea Harrier FR21s, US Marine Corps AV-8As and AV-8Bs, and Indian, Italian, and Spanish aircraft.

In 1992, re-branded as the 20 (Reserve) Squadron, for 18 years it taught a new generation of pilots to fly the GR5/7/9 variants. In 2020 the squadron relocated to RAF Cottesmore as part of Joint Force Harrier and began to teach Royal Navy pilots to fly the GR7 and GR9 after the retirement of the Sea Harrier FA2.

The Harrier OCU role was taken over by the renamed IV (Reserve) Squadron in March 2010.

Unit: 20 Squadron (1970-77), 233 OCU (1977-1992), 20 (Reserve) Squadron (1992-2010)
Nickname/Motto: Facta non verba (Deeds not Words)
Home Base: RAF Wittering (1970-1977, 1992-2010)

Aircraft
Harrier GR1/3: 1969-1994
Harrier GR5/7/7A: 1987-2006
Harrier GR9/9A: 2006-2010

207 SQUADRON

The United Kingdom Lightning Force (UKLF) operates the F-35B Lightning II combat jet from RAF Marham in Norfolk, where the flying squadrons, training and maintenance elements are all based. This is a fully integrated unit with mixed RAF and Royal Navy air and ground crew; personnel from both services are mixed into the flying squadrons, training, and support elements.

The second RAF unit assigned to the UK, 207 Squadron was formed in the summer of 2019 after the arrival of the first F-35Bs at RAF Marham. As the UK operational conversion unit, the majority of RAF and Royal Navy F-35B pilots will carry out their conversion to type training with the squadron, although a handful receive instruction in the US.

A full suite of simulators has been installed at RAF Marham to allow students to carry out an intensive training before taking to the skies in a real F-35B. As there is no two-seat variant of the jet, this phase of the training is crucial to the successful conversion of pilots.

A major focus is on generating aircrew with the necessary qualifications to fly off aircraft carriers, so each year student pilots undertake short deployments on board one of the vessels. On January 28, 2020, 207 Squadron became the first UK unit in a decade to operate jets in home waters from a British carrier, flying from HMS *Queen Elizabeth*.

Unit: 207 Squadron
Nickname/Motto: Semper paratus (Always prepared)
Home Base: RAF Marham

Aircraft
F-35: 2017 to date

617 SQUADRON 'DAMBUSTERS'

evaluation unit, 617 Squadron is often lined up for high profile tasks that would attract publicity and has been designated as the lead unit to bring new equipment or capabilities into service.

In 1962, it was the first Vulcan squadron to be equipped with the stand-off Blue Steel nuclear missile. During the 1991 Gulf War, it played an important role in the TIALD task force, which used the targeting pod to direct laser-guided bomb. During the 2003 Iraq invasion, it operationally fired the first MBDA Storm Shadow air-launched cruise missile.

More recently, it was the lead squadron to bring the F-35B Lightning II into service, before taking the jets to sea for the first time on an operational cruise embarked on HMS *Queen Elizabeth* in 2021.

The squadron was disbanded in 2014 after retiring its Panavia Tornado GR4 strike jets, after which personnel started to train on the F-35B in the US from 2016. Formally reformed in April 2018, the new 617 Squadron and its first four F-35Bs arrived at their new home at RAF Marham in June 2018 after flying across the Atlantic. It was declared operational in January 2019 and, later in the year, flew its first operational mission over Syria from RAF Akrotiri, Cyprus.

Unit: 617 Squadron
Nickname/Motto: The Dambusters; Après moi le déluge (After me, the flood)
Home Base: RAF Marham

Aircraft
F-35B: 2018 to date

Undoubtedly the RAF's most famous squadron thanks to its role in the famous World War Two mission to attack German dams under the command of Wing Commander Guy Gibson VC. Although not formally a test and

ROYAL NAVY
800 NAVAL AIR SQUADRON

Originally formed in 1933, 800 Naval Air Squadron (NAS) saw distinguished service during World War Two, including joining the carrier strike on the Nazi battleship *Tirpitz* in 1944. It also took part in Korean War and, in the 1960s and early 1970s, flew the iconic Blackburn Buccaneer strike jet.

The squadron was the first Fleet Air Arm unit to convert to the Sea Harrier FRS1 and, in 1982, embarked on HMS *Hermes* for Operation Corporate, the mission to liberate the Falkland Islands.

Under the command of Lieutenant Commander Andy Auld, the squadron operated from HMS *Hermes* for the duration of the Falklands conflict. Two of the squadron's planes were lost, one when it exploded on take-off from HMS *Hermes,* and one shot down during an attack on Goose Green. No Harriers were lost in air-to-air combat, and the squadron is credited with destroying 13 enemy aircraft. It continued to operate the FRS1 until the mid-1990s when it converted to the FA2 variant. During the late 1990s, it flew missions over the Iraq no-fly zone from HMS *Illustrious* as part of the newly formed Joint Force Harrier.

Briefly disbanded in 2004, 800 NAS reformed in 2006 to fly the Harrier GR7 and GR9. In 2007, it was combined with 801 NAS to form the Naval Strike Wing but, in April 2010, it returned to the designation 800 NAS.

After the October 2010 Strategic Defence Review decided to scrap the Harrier, 800 NAS was disbanded for a final time.

Unit: 800 Naval Air Squadron, Naval Strike Wing (2007-2010)
Nickname/Motto: Nunquam non-paratus *(*Never unprepared)
Home Base: RNAS Yeovilton (1980-2004), RAF Cottesmore (2006-2010)

Aircraft
Sea Harrier FRS1 (1980-1993)
Sea Harrier FA2 (1993-2004)
Harrier GR9 (2006-2010)

801 NAVAL AIR SQUADRON

ABOVE: 801 Naval Air Squadron shows off its Sea Harrier FA2s.
MoD/Crown Copyright

Serving with distinction during World War Two and the Korean War, 801 NAS operated the Blackburn Buccaneer in the Far East in the 1960s, before disbanding in the 1970s. In January 1981, the squadron re-equipped with the Sea Harrier FRS1 at RNAS Yeovilton and, a year later, embarked on HMS *Invincible* for Operation Corporate, under the command of the legendary Lieutenant Commander 'Sharkey' Ward.

The squadron was in the thick of the action in the Falklands, claiming eight Argentine aircraft shot down. It lost three aircraft and pilots in accidents and one jet was shot down by an Argentinian Roland surface-to-air missile, but the pilot was rescued. In 1994, one of its Sea Harrier FRS1s was shot down over Bosnia and the pilot spent several days in the besieged city of Gorazde before being rescued.

The squadron operated the Sea Harrier FA2 until 2006, when the jet was retired on cost grounds, making it the last British operator of an all-British combat aircraft. There were plans to reform the squadron in 2007 to operate the Harrier GR9, but its personnel were instead transferred to the new Naval Strike Wing.

Unit: 801 Naval Air Squadron
Nickname/Motto: On Les Aura (We'll have them)
Home Base: RNAS Yeovilton (1981-2006)

Aircraft
Sea Harrier FRS1: 1981-1993
Sea Harrier FA2: 1993-2006

RIGHT: When the Sea Harrier FA2 was retired in 2006, 801 Naval Air Squadron was disbanded.
MoD/Crown Copyright

809 NAVAL AIR SQUADRON

RIGHT: 809 Naval Air Squadron was reborn to fly the F-35B in December 2023 as part of the UK Lightning Force at RAF Marham.
MoD/Crown Copyright

force, the jets transferred to HMS *Hermes* and HMS *Invincible*, with four aircraft going to each carrier, where they were absorbed into 800 and 801 NAS. They remained recognisable as they had been painted in light grey low-visibility camouflage as opposed to the dark sea grey scheme used by the other Sea Harriers.

Post-Falklands, 809 NAS reacquired its aircraft and crews, returning to the UK alongside 800 NAS aboard HMS *Hermes*, only to make a rapid turnaround to be ready to embark aboard the newly completed HMS *Illustrious* as she headed to the Falklands to relieve HMS *Invincible*. The squadron disbanded in December 1982 on the carrier's return to the UK.

In December 2023, 809 NAS was resurrected as the Royal Navy's contribution to the UK Lightning Force, flying the F-35B Lightning II.

BELOW: RAF and Royal Navy pilots serve in 809 Naval Air Squadron at RAF Marham under the joint UK Lightning Force.
MoD/Crown Copyright

Formed in 1941, 809 Naval Air Squadron saw heavy action for the remainder of World War Two. It took part in the 1956 Suez crisis, then flew the Blackburn Buccaneer until it was disbanded in 1978, when the aircraft were transferred to the RAF.

The squadron was briefly reformed during the 1982 Falklands conflict to take over spare aircraft mustered to reinforce the squadrons already in the South Atlantic, embarking on the converted civilian container ship MV *Atlantic Conveyor*. Once she was within range of the Royal Navy task

Unit: 809 Naval Air Squadron
Nickname/Motto: The Immortals
Home Base: RNAS Yeovilton (1982), RAF Marham (2023 to date)

Aircraft
Sea Harrier FRS1: 1982
F-35B: 2023 to date

899 NAVAL AIR SQUADRON

For 25 years, 899 NAS was the Sea Harrier operational conversion unit, based at RNAS Culdrose. It traces its roots back to 1942, when it was formed to fly the Supermarine Seafire IIC. After operations in the Mediterranean, it was transferred to the Pacific as part of the ramping up of British aircraft carrier campaign against the Japanese. The squadron was in the vanguard of the introduction of jet fighters into the Fleet Air Arm in the 1950s, operating the Hawker Sea Hawk and de Haviland Sea Vixen.

As part of the project to bring the Sea Harrier FRS1 into service after 1980, 899 NAS was designated the type's operational conversion unit (OCU). During the 1982 Falklands conflict, many of its personnel and aircraft were dispatched to the South Atlantic.

In the OCU role, it operated the FAA's two-seat Sea Harriers, first with the T4 variant and, from the 1995, the T8, which was a version of the FA2. The decision to retire the Sea Harrier from service in 2004 and for the FAA to share the GR7/9 fleet with the RAF led to

the disbandment of the dedicated OCU in March 2005. After this, Royal Navy Harrier pilots trained with their RAF counterparts in 20 Squadron at RAF Cottesmore until the Harrier was withdrawn from service in 2010.

Unit: 899 Naval Air Squadron
Nickname/Motto: Strike and defend
Home Base: RNAS Yeovilton

Aircraft
Sea Harrier FRS1: 1980-1993
Sea Harrier FA2: 1993 -2005

BELOW: 899 Naval Air Squadron was the Sea Harrier operational conversion unit from 1980 to 2005. Britpilot

UNITED STATES MARINE CORPS
VMFA-121

Marine Fighter Attack Squadron 121 was previously an F/A-18D Hornet unit, before converting to the F/A-35B Lightning II in 2012, becoming the first USMC squadron to operate the type. In 2017, it relocated from MCAS Yuma to MCAS Iwakuni in Japan, where it supported units based in the Far East, including providing small detachments onboard amphibious landing ships.

After being formed in 1941, the squadron saw action in the Pacific during World War Two, Korea and Vietnam.

Unit: VMFA-121
Nickname: Green Knights
Tail Code: VK
Home Base: MCAS Iwakuni

Aircraft
F-35B: 2012 to date

RIGHT: F-35Bs assigned to VMFA 121 landed on the amphibious assault ship USS *Wasp* in 2018, marking the first time the type had deployed aboard a US Navy ship and with a marine expeditionary unit in the Indo-Pacific region. US DoD/ Combat Camera

HARRIER AND LIGHTNING SQUADRONS

Initially, from the 1970s to the 1990s, frontline marine attack squadrons (VMAs) were each allocated 20 AV-8A/C/Bs. By 2002, the strength of USMC Harrier squadrons was reduced to 15 aircraft, with a mix of AV-8B Plus and AV-8N Night Attack variants.

The USMC currently has a mix of marine fighter attack squadrons (VMFAs) equipped with 10 or 16 F-35Bs, but by 2035 all units will have transitioned to a 12-jet structure. All USMC Harrier and Lightning squadrons are configured to deploy as complete units or provide six to eight jet detachments to serve with marine expeditionary units on amphibious assault ships.

There are currently eight operational F-35B squadrons, with four more to form by 2032. These include two AV-8B squadrons (VMA-231 and 223) and two F/A-18C/Ds units (VMFA-224 and 312).

RIGHT: Two USMC squadrons still fly the AV-8B, but they will all be retired by 2027. US DoD/ Combat Camera

VMFA-122

The former McDonnell Douglas F/A-18C Hornet squadron began converting to the Lockheed Martin F-35B Lightning II in October 2017 and, a year later, was declared operational as the third USMC to fly the new jump jet.

The squadron has a distinguished history, stretching back to 1942, when it was formed to fly the iconic F4F Wildcat, then transitioned to the F4U Corsair. In 1947, it became the first USMC air squadrons to fly jet-powered FH Phantoms.

It converted from F-4 Phantoms to single-seat Hornets in 1986, taking the jets to war in Iraq in 2003 and 2008, before heading to Afghanistan in 2010.

Unit: VMFA-122
Nickname: Flying Leathernecks
Tail Code: DC
Home Base: MCAS Yuma

Aircraft
F-35B: 2018 to date

VMAT-203

Marine Attack Training Squadron 203 has been the home of Harrier aircrew and maintenance personnel training since 1975, when it transitioned from the A-4 Skyhawk to the AV-8A. Based at MCAS Cherry Point in North Carolina, the unit also operated two-seat TAV-8A versions of the Harrier to convert pilots to fly the jump jet.

AV-8B Harrier IIs started arriving at VMAT-203 in December 1983, and the old A model aircraft had been retired by 1985. The squadron continued to teach AV-8B pilots and maintainers until November 2021, when it was disbanded and reduced to Fleet Replacement Detachment to train the dwindling number of Harrier personnel as the jump jet moved towards retirement. The final two pilots completed AV-8B conversion in April 2024.

Unit: VMAT-203
Nickname: Hawks
Tail Code: KD
Home Base: MCAS Cherry Point

Aircraft
AV-8A: 1975-1987
AV-8B: 1987-2021

TAV-8As of VMAT-203 were used to train Harrier pilots from 1975. US DoD/Combat Camera

VMFA-211

The Wake Island Avengers currently fly the F-35B.
US DoD/Combat Camera

Marine Fighter Attack Squadron 211 is one of the most distinguished USMC aviation units, with a history stretching back to 1937. It was famously assigned to defend the beleaguered Pacific Island of Wake in the face of an overwhelming Japanese invasion force during World War Two.

The squadron converted from the A-4 Skyhawk to the AV-8B in 1990 and operated the Harrier II for 16 more years. It became the second USMC squadron to convert to the F-35B Lightning II and, in 2018, was the first F-35B unit to drop bombs in anger. In 2021 it spent more than six months embarked on the British aircraft carrier HMS *Queen Elizabeth* for her deployment to the Mediterranean, Indian Ocean, and Pacific region.

Unit: VMA-211, VMFA-211 (from 2016)
Nickname: Wake Island Avengers
Tail Code: CF
Home Base: MCAS Yuma

Aircraft
AV-8B: 1990-2016
F-35B: 2016 to date

VMFA-214

The famous 'Black Sheep' squadron was formed in 1942 and thrown into the Soloman Islands campaign against the Japanese, winning a Presidential Unit Citation for extraordinary heroism in action. It flew the A-4 Skyhawk from 1962 to 1997, when it converted to fly the night attack variant of the AV-8B Harrier II. It missed the 1991 Gulf War as it was still becoming fully qualified in night attack tactics.

In March 2022, the squadron was redesignated as Marine Fighter Attack Squadron 214 and began receiving the F-35B Lightning II.

Unit: VMA-214, VMFA-214
Nickname: The Black Sheep
Tail Code: WE
Home Base: MCAS Yuma

Aircraft
AV-8B: 1989-2022
F-35B: 2022 to date

VMFA-214 began converting to the F-35B in 2022.
US DoD/Combat Camera

VMA-223

After being formed in 1942, the F4F Wildcats of VMF-223 were the first fighters committed to combat during the Battle of Guadalcanal, having landed at Henderson Field in August 1942. In 1987, it traded in its A-4 Skyhawks for the AV-8B Harrier II. The squadron didn't take part in the 1991 Gulf War but was embarked on USS *Bataan* for the invasion of Iraq in 2003. It still operates the AV-8B and is expected to be the last USMC unit to operate the type.

VMA-223 is expected to be the last USMC squadron to fly the AV-8B.
US DoD/Combat Camera

Unit: VMA-223
Nickname: Bulldogs
Tail Code: WP
Home Base: MCAS Cherry Point

Aircraft
AV-8B: 1987 to date (including Harrier II Plus)

VMFA-225

VMFA-225 converted to fly the F-35B from the F/A-18D.
US DoD/Combat Camera

Marine Fighting Squadron 225 was commissioned in January 1942 and its F4U Corsairs participated in numerous combat operations in the New Hebrides Islands campaign. During the Vietnam war, it flew the A-6A Intruder in the battlefield air interdiction role and then transitioned to the two-seat F/A-18D Hornet. From January 2021, it started to convert to fly the F-35B Lightning II as a marine fighter attack squadron, supporting Pacific Fleet-aligned USMC units.

Unit: VMFA-225
Nickname: Vikings
Tail Code: CE
Home Base: MCAS Yuma

Aircraft
F-35B: 2021 to date

VMA-231

The Ace of Spades can trace its history back to World War One, when it was one of the first US Marine Corps aviation units.
Paul Maritz

Marine Attack Squadron 231 can trace its history back to the first USMC aviation units in World War One. The unit opened a new chapter in 1973, when it was reformed as one of the three original AV-8A operators. In 1984, it transitioned to the AV-8B Harrier II, flying the aircraft with distinction during the 1991 and 2003 Gulf Wars. It also carried out deployments to Iraq and Afghanistan for counter-insurgency operations in 2007 and 2009, respectively.

The squadron is one of the last two still flying the AV-8B and is expected to begin converting to the F-35B Lightning II in 2026.

Unit: VMA-231
Nickname: Ace of Spades
Tail Code: CG
Home Base: MCAS Cherry Point

Aircraft
AV-8A: 1973-1984
AV-8B: 1984 to date (including Harrier II Plus)
F-35B: From 2026

VMFA-242

Starting out in World War Two as a torpedo bomber unit, Marine Fighter Attack Squadron 242 served in that role until 1964, when it transitioned to the battlefield air interdiction A-6A Intruder, then to the two-seat F/A-18D Hornet in 1990. In 2020, it began to convert to the F-35B Lightning II. On October 3, 2021, two VMFA-242 jets landed on the Japanese carrier JS *Izumo*, the first time since World War Two that fixed-wing aircraft had operated off a Japanese warship.

Unit: VMFA-242
Nickname: Bats
Tail Code: DT
Home Base: MCAS Iwakuni

Aircraft
F-35B: 2020 to date

VMFA-242 is forward based in Japan to operate in the Western Pacific region.
US DoD/Combat Camera

VMA-311

Tracing its history back to 1942, Marine Attack Squadron 311 was formed as a ground attack unit, flying the F4U Corsair. The squadron received the AV-8B Harrier II in 1998 and, two years later, was the first USMC AV-8B unit to deploy to the Middle East during the build up to the 1991 Gulf War. It saw action over in the Gulf again in 2003 during the invasion of Iraq.

Part of the USMC Tactical Aviation transition to the F-35 Lightning II, the squadron disbanded in 2020, but did not re-form as F-35B unit, instead standing up again in 2023 to operate the F-35C.

Unit: VMA-311
Nickname: Tomcats
Tail Code: WL
Home Base: MCAS Yuma

Aircraft
AV-8B: 1989-2020

VMA-311 led the charge in Operation Desert Storm as the first USMC Harrier squadron to deploy to Saudi Arabia in August 1990.
US DoD/Combat Camera

VMA-331

Marine Attack Squadron 331 was formed in 1943 and supported the USMC's island-hopping campaign, including amphibious landings on Tarawa and the Marshal Islands. The squadron was the first USMC unit to become fully operational in the AV-8B Harrier II. It deployed on the USS *Nassau* during the 1991 Gulf War and was the first marine attack squadron to conduct combat operations from an amphibious assault ship. It was disbanded in October 1992 as part of the post-Cold War drawdown of the US military.

Unit: VMA-331
Nickname: Bumblebees
Tail Code: VL
Home Base: MCAS Beaufort

Aircraft
AV-8B: 1983-1992

A round of defence budget cuts after the end of the Cold War led to the disbanding of VMA-331 in 1992.
US DoD/Combat Camera

VMFAT-501

VMFAT-501 is the F-35B fleet replenishment squadron on the US east coast. US DoD/Combat Camera

One of two fleet replenishment squadrons converting pilots to fly the F-35B Lightning II, Marine Fighter Attack Training Squadron 501 has adopted the history of the MFS 451, which was originally formed in 1944 to fly the F4U-1D Corsair. MFS 451 was deactivated in 1997 and was re-formed in April 2010 as VMFAT-501 at the National Museum of Naval Aviation at Naval Air Station Pensacola, Florida. It was initially stationed at Eglin Air Force Base in Florida, where the first cadre of F-35 pilots from the USAF, US Navy and USMC were trained, before moving to its permanent home at MCAS Beaufort in South Carolina in July 2014.

Unit: VMFAT-501
Nickname: Vin Vici/Warhawks/Blue Devils/Fightin' Phillies
Tail Code: BM/VM
Home Base: Elgin AFV (2010-2014), MCAS Beaufort (from 2014)

Aircraft
F-35B: 2010 to date

VMFAT-502

During World War Two, Marine Attack Squadron 513 fought during the invasion of Okinawa in 1945 that saw US Marines capture the first territory of the Japanese homeland. In 1971, the squadron became the initial USMC unit to operate the AV-8A Harrier. It began receiving the AV-8B Harrier II in 1987 and deployed to the Arabian Gulf onboard the USS *Tarawa* in 1991. It was disbanded in 2013 as part of the rundown of the AV-8B fleet. In 2020, Marine Fighter Attack Training Squadron 502 was formed as the fleet replenishment unit to convert pilots to fly the F-35B Lightning II, when it adopted the history and traditions of VMA-513.

Unit: VMA-513, VMFAT-502 (from 2020)
Nickname: Flying Nightmares
Tail Code: WF
Home Base: MCAS Yuma (until 2013), NAS Miramar (from 2020)

Aircraft
AV-8A: 1971-1987
AV-8B: 1987-2013
F-35B: 2020 to date

VMFAT-502 has adopted the history of VMA-513, the first USMC unit to convert to the Harrier in 1971. US DoD/Combat Camera

VMFA-533

Marine Fighter Attack Squadron 533 can trace its history back to 1943, when it was formed as a night attack unit with the F6F-5N Hellcat equipped with the APS-6 radar. Before deploying to Vietnam in 1967, the squadron converted to the A-6A Intruder and, in 1992, the two-seat F/A-18D Hornet arrived. The unit was heavily engaged in the 2003 invasion of Iraq. The squadron handed in its Hornets in 2023 and started to convert to the F-35B Lightning II. This process is still underway and, when fully operational, VMFA-553 will be the first operational F-35B unit at MCAS Beaufort.

Unit: VMFA-533
Nickname: Hawks
Tail Code: ED
Home Base: MCAS Beaufort

Aircraft
F-35B: 2023 to date

VMFA-533 is in the process of transitioning to the F-35B at MCAS Beaufort. US DoD/ Combat Camera

VMFA-542

Dating back to 1944, Marine Fighter Attack Squadron 542 was re-formed in 1972 as the USMC's second AV-AB Harrier operator. It flew the AV-8A/C until 1986, when the squadron began to convert to the AV-8B. During the build-up to the 1991 Gulf War, it was the first unit to receive the radar-equipped AV-8B Plus variant. The squadron retired its last Harriers in December 2022 and began transitioning to the F-35B Lightning II.

Unit: VMFA-542
Nickname: Tigers
Tail Code: WH
Home Base: MCAS Cherry Point

Aircraft
AV-8A: 1972-1987
AV-8B: 1987-2024 (including Harrier II Plus)
F-35B: 2022 to date

VMA-542 was the second USMC unit to convert to AV-8A and, in 1982, embarked on the USS *Nassau*. US Navy

THE LEGACY OF THE JUMP JET AND ITS FUTURE

How VTOL jets have transformed aerial combat

The Harrier jump jet has always been an aircraft that caught people's attention, particularly at airshows in the 1960s and 1970s. Several air arms immediately saw the potential of vertical take-off and landing aircraft and began making moves to buy the Harrier or develop their own. The 1982 Falklands war turned the Harrier from being an airshow star into a battle winner.

Royal Navy Sea Harrier pilots defeated the Argentinian air force and RAF GR3 ground attack pilots devastated the land army. The ability of the jump jets to deploy from small aircraft carriers in dreadful weather was remarkable and showed that naval airpower did not have to rely on large 'cats and traps' super carriers to be highly effective. Then RAF

LEFT: The Sea Harrier demonstrated the combat-effectiveness of the jump jet during the 1982 Falklands War and played a major part in the British victory.
MoD/Crown Copyright

BELOW: The F-35B Lightning II is now the world's only jump jet still in production.
MoD/Crown Copyright

LEFT: HMS *Hermes* was the flagship of the Royal Navy's Falklands Task Force and continued to operate Sea Harriers after being sold to the Indian Navy as INS *Viraat*.
MoD/Crown Copyright

Harrier pilots took their jets ashore to operate from improvised airstrips cut into the side of a beach or in the middle of a jungle or in congested urban areas.

At the time of the Falklands crisis, the USMC was already working on the next generation of jump jet, the AV-8B Harrier II, and they took it to war in large numbers during Operation Desert Storm in 1991. Day after day in the skies over Kuwait, USMC AV-8B pilots proved themselves to be outstanding close air support experts. By operating from austere desert locations, the USMC jump jets were always close to the action and ready to respond for calls for help from their 'ground pounding' comrades in USMC infantry units.

They repeated this in the 2003 invasion of Iraq and then again in Afghanistan, but modern targeting pods supported by ROVER terminals that allowed them to strike targets with pinpoint accuracy. In counter-insurgency campaigns, in which victory was achieved by winning 'hearts and minds' of civilians, precision strikes with low collateral damage were the order of the day.

USMC Harrier squadrons demonstrated time after time that their expertise at close air support throughout the so-called 'global war on terror'. They took their jets to remote locations, got them in the air and kept fighting despite hurdles that would have grounded other aviation units. When Camp Bastion's perimeter fence was breached in 2012, the 'Wake Island Avengers' reached for their rifles and fought off the Taliban attackers. Within days they were back in the air over Afghanistan, providing close air support for their comrades across Helmand Province.

The second-generation Harrier was adopted by the British, Italian, and Spanish, who used it to great effect in wars in the Balkans, Middle East, and Africa. RAF GR7s and GR9s proved rugged and effective jets, and their pilots won their spurs as Britain's close air support experts in several campaigns. The British modified their Harriers throughout the 1990s and into the 21st Century to keep the jets relevant to modern threats. The Sea Harrier FA2 brought beyond-visual-range capabilities to Royal Navy aircraft carriers and the precision-guided weapons of the GR9 won the jet much praise from troops in Afghanistan.

The basic concept for the Harrier, which used its four rotating exhausts to generate lift, was so simple and effective that, for a long time, it could not be matched, let alone beaten. Attempts by the Soviet Navy to »

BELOW: The USMC's AV-8B wrote several chapters of jump jet history in conflicts around the world.
US DoD/Combat Camera

produce their own jump jet, the Yakovlev Yak-38, were not a success. It saw service on Soviet aircraft carriers in the 1970s and 1980s but never won any export orders and the Red Air Force did not select it. In the one head-to-head contest between a Harrier and a Yak-38 in India, the FRS1 won easily. The Indian navy did not even move to a formal competition – they wanted the Sea Harrier. No contest.

Over the past decade, the Harrier has started to give way to the latest generation of jump jet, the F-35B Lightning II, with its revolutionary lift fan. This combines stealth technology with advanced weapons, with the ability to take-off and land vertically. It's the jump jet for the 21st Century and is expected to see service well beyond 2050. As the only jump jet in mass production, the F-35B is attracting interest from navies around the world that want to refresh their naval airpower or get into the aircraft carrier game for the first time.

Britain and Italy have successfully put the F-35B to sea on their new generation of aircraft carriers. Japan is getting back in the carrier business after an 80-year break by buying the F-35B to be embarked on its two new flat-tops. Spain is looking to replace its Harriers with F-35Bs, but

funding issues are delaying its order, which might make the Spanish Navy the last ever operator of the Harrier by the time it retires circa 2030. South Korea and Singapore are both mulling ordering the F-35B to embark on their amphibious assault ships.

This would expand the jump jet club considerably.

Where does the jump jet go from here? The F-35B era is only just beginning and operators are only just working out what the jet can do and how to exploit its unique

ABOVE: Italy and Spain were two export customers of the AV-8B Plus and Spain is set to be last Harrier II operator after the USMC retires its jump jets in 2027.
US DoD/Combat Camera

RIGHT: Many USMC Harrier squadrons can trace their heritage back to World War Two, flying F4U Corsairs against the Japanese.
US DoD/Combat Camera

features to best effect. However, the advent of unmanned technology to create swarms of drones offers new potential for vertical flight. Drones do not require large runways, and many are small enough to operate from remote locations. This means drones offer many of the advantages and benefits of jump jets, without the cost and risks of putting human pilots in them.

It is perhaps too soon to write the obituary on the manned jump jet. Despite many of the claims for the ability of artificial intelligence (AI) to outthink humans, flesh and blood pilots will still have a place in the cockpits of future jump jets. Humans can still make split-second decisions that are needed to win in air combat or overcome mechanical breakdowns.

For more than 60 years, jump jet pilots have shown themselves »

ABOVE: 801 Naval Air Squadron retired the Sea Harrier FA2 in 2005 with a celebratory flypast of HMS *Illustrious*.
MoD/Crown Copyright

RIGHT: The RAF and Royal Navy said farewell to the Harrier in 2010 when a round of defence cost cutting forced the early retirement of the jump jets.
MoD/Crown Copyright

RIGHT: The USMC started flying the F-35B in 2012 to begin its transition from the AV-8B. US DoD/Combat Camera

BELOW: The UK Lightning Force expects to fly the F-35B from the Royal Navy's two Queen Elizabeth-class carriers beyond 2050. MoD/Crown Copyright

to be resourceful, determined and highly effective military aviators. Yes, the Harrier and its derivatives have been superb aircraft, with many battle-winning features, but it has been the pilots that have won the day on numerous occasions. The old military maxim – 'adapt, improvise, overcome' – could have been written for Harrier pilots who turned out to be a special breed of aviator. It is now up to future generations of F-35B pilots to pick up the baton and write new chapters in the history of the jump jet.

The Harrier will be a tough act to follow.